WHO ARE YOU

BECOMING?

D1518469

JONATHAN FANNING

WHO ARE YOU BECOMING?

FIRST EDITION
Copyright ©2014 Jonathan Fanning

ISBN
9798609280329

Cover Design: Rebecca Lazaroff

For more information on this title and other books, videos, CDs, seminars, and speaking engagements, please visit:
www.JonathanFanning.com

Printed in the United States of America.

Contents

Prologue

Perhaps we have quite a bit in common. I've been hit over the head by many frying pans in my life. All too often, I have felt the lesson, heard the lesson, reflected on the lesson, and then applied very little of the lesson – until another similar frying pan struck me in the same place, maybe even a bit harder. I've climbed ladders that were not mine to climb. Stood part of the way or most of the way up one of these ladders, looked around, and realized this particular ladder was not one that I should be climbing. Then, I would often look down to see how many rungs I had already climbed, and try to rationalize staying on this ladder, despite knowing that it was not the right ladder for me.

I've poured my time, energy, focus, and life into climbing these ladders and into trying to ignore the frying pans. I've felt tremendous clarity around my life's purpose for a few fleeting moments and then tried to chase down that clarity with attempts which felt as futile as my three-year-old chasing fireflies without a net.

I have felt the restlessness that Augustine described in the 4th century.

I've consulted for some of the biggest companies in the world, started several businesses, considered joining the non-profit world, and questioned the meaning of just about everything. I've been successful and unsuccessful. Felt tremendous joy and peace as well as their opposites. Through all this, I've tried to learn lessons from legends in many arenas. I believe in serving others. I believe that some of my story can help you in your journey.

Thank you for the chance to add value to your life!

Jonathan Fanning

Chapter 1

The Question

Hanging from a bridge 106 feet above the ground should wake you up.

That first March weekend was unusually warm. It was a great weekend for our family's annual birthday experience. My mother, father, and younger brother, Peter, all have birthdays within 10 days of each other. As you can imagine, each year, this annual gathering has become a family tradition. This year, my older brother, Andrew, his girlfriend, Monica, and I were living just outside Detroit, so we made the 8 hour road trip to Northeast Pennsylvania together that Friday night. After a very busy weekend and a gorgeous Sunday afternoon spent playing basketball in the driveway, catching up with cousins, and eating second and third helpings of homemade lasagna, we begrudgingly got in the car around 5pm to begin the return voyage. To make these trips bearable, we would rotate drivers, usually just once to minimize the stops and total travel time.

Just a few hours into the trip, a light rain had begun to fall and Andrew fell asleep, as he so often did, in the back seat. I refrained from asking Monica to drive a little faster, although I kept noting the time, mileage, and speed; rapidly calculating our probable arrival time and thinking about how excited I would not be on Monday morning when the alarm sounded. The falling rain became steadier and our headlights lit just enough of the roadway to keep us hypnotized. At about 8 pm, without warning, the car started sliding sideways towards the 3 foot concrete barrier to our left. Monica screamed and struggled to keep us from careening off the barrier. My brother, Andrew lurched awake, tilting his body up just in time to see us bounce off the left barrier and spin into the middle of the road. The first tractor trailer slammed into our car, impacting our back driver's side, projecting Andrew's head into the column between the side windows. Our car spun the opposite direction. Time froze as I stared, horrified, through my window at a second tractor trailer, this one older with a dull red cab, as it crashed directly into my door.

I don't remember losing consciousness, but do very clearly recall leaning away and bracing for the impact.

Finally, our car stopped sliding. We were still on the highway and facing the right direction, in the left lane with a white delivery van and several other cars proceeding towards us. Kicking the door seemed futile, but after a few good solid kicks, the door – or whatever remained of it – flung open. I stood outside the car for what seemed a long time but must have been just an instant and stared through the broken back window at my big brother – just 20 months older than I – unconscious and with a pool of blood around his head. Panic overwhelmed me. The white van was sliding towards me. Realizing it would not hit the car, but was going to hit me, I bolted towards the right side of the road and decided to leap the concrete barrier. Why did I pause? Why? "Don't jump." I felt a quiet but firm urge not to jump over that barrier. I quickly climbed over instead. On the other side of the barrier, my feet found nothing to stand on. Nothing.

Nothing. Hanging from the concrete barrier, I leaned back as the white van slid by, coming dangerously close to my arms as

2

they clung to the barrier. The next few cars slowed and passed by. I pulled myself back over the barrier and my feet found the ground once again. Stumbling towards the car, I arrived to see my brother, Andrew, regaining consciousness. He tried to speak, but only unintelligible words came out. His face was already swelling, disfigured, and bleeding. I ran down the road towards the white van and cars which had stopped after sliding past us. As I stumbled, I kept yelling "Somebody help my brother! My brother! Help! Help!" Then I stumbled, fell, and collapsed on the side of the road. How had I found the energy to hold on to that concrete barrier just minutes before?

Getting loaded into the ambulance and the few miles travel to Clarion Hospital seemed to take several hours. Get us strapped down already. Get my brother to safety. He needs to live! My big brother! The beeping sound monitoring his heart kept mine racing. Would he make it?

Get us to the hospital.

GET US TO THE HOSPITAL!

I don't think I had even felt any pain up to this point. But a deep profound sorrow accompanied with a tremendous sense of urgency was taking over my whole being. Upon arrival at the hospital, the three of us, Monica, Andrew, and I were separated. By the time I saw my brother again, the pain throughout my own body had become an intense throbbing coupled with uncontrollable shivering. Andrew was in a neck brace. His brain was swelling and his skull shattered all around his left eye and cheek. He would be airlifted via helicopter to Pittsburgh immediately.

A doctor gave me a phone to call my parents. I could barely tell them what was happening though, between my shivering, trembling voice and sobbing. My mother's first response: "You made it home. Don't kid like this. You're fine and back in Michigan." No, Mom. No. We are not alright. I don't know what's going to happen with Andrew. I couldn't stay on the phone. My parents immediately followed our same route to Clarion, picked up Monica and me, and we continued on to meet up with Andrew at the University of Pittsburgh's Medical Center.

A week in the hospital, reflecting on almost losing a brother and hanging off of a bridge gets you thinking about life. What is it all about? What if ours had ended that day? Had we truly lived our lives? Had we lived OUR lives? Was there more? Why? Will I do anything differently with this second chance? I made a decision that very week that the direction of my life would change. Life really was a precious commodity and I had not been living my priorities. The journey had been in pursuit of a set of goals, values, lifestyle. Now

> "If you want to identify me, ask me not where I live, or what I like to eat, or how I comb my hair, but ask me what I am living for, in detail, ask me what I think is keeping me from living fully for the thing I want to live for."
> ~ Thomas Merton

that was all in vain. I had a new direction. Is that possible? Can you change the direction of your life in a few days? As a result of one – albeit very significant and emotional – event? What would I change? Just about everything. Work. Family. Life. Relationships. Who I was as a person. What I did for a living – more than "did" – dedicated – no gave – my life to. It would all change. Some changes would be radical, others minor, but there were changes to be made. And now was the time. It could have been all over. Instead, I would borrow a phrase from Winston Churchill: "History will be kind to me for I intend to write it." Have you experienced this?

Somehow, two years had passed and that big family birthday weekend was approaching. My brother had recovered and you couldn't even tell that he had been involved in an accident. I thought back on that day and the week in hospitals that followed. Then I looked at my two years of changing everything. Everything in my life had changed. Everything. Wait... how had this happened? Everything that had changed was simply a facade. Nothing had really changed in my life. Yes, I changed jobs that very week. Yes, I physically moved 550 miles east to live near those that mattered most to me. Yes, I said I stood for something different now. All this and nothing had really changed. Different career but the same. Different schedule but the same. How? How had this happened? Better questions were starting to make their way into my life.

Who am I BECOMING?

100 years from today, what ripple effect will my life have created?

The bridge on Interstate 80 in Clarion, Pennsylvania is about 106 feet above the ground. On the right guardrail on the westbound lane, travelers still see marks left from this night.

That bridge in the mountains of western Pennsylvania changed the direction of my life, started the seed of a new vision in my heart, mind, and soul. A few years after, however, not much had changed. My habits of behavior and thought weren't much different. I often ask friends, casual acquaintances, and audiences this simple question: How do you want your life to be different a year from now than it is today? Will you build your life around the answer?

How big a frying pan do you really need?

Maybe we all have wandering phases in our lives? Is it a necessary part of the journey? If so, is there any way we can shorten the aimless wandering for future generations? Someone wise must have handled this question before. More on that later.

How I met the Benedictine Monk Antonio is a different question, all together, and perhaps the topic of another book or two. Like so many of life's greatest lessons, this chance encounter that turned into a friendship and mentorship happened without my conscious pursuit or permission. A friend I hadn't seen since high school invited me to dinner at his small graduate student apartment. I've never been known to turn down a home-cooked meal and my friend's unique visitor who was rapidly preparing a Tuscan sausage soup dish certainly seemed to know his way around the kitchen. Brother Antonio is from Calabria, the region of Italy that he claims is famous for being able to make a delicious meal out of dirt. As the random ingredients almost instantly turned into an irresistible bubbling meal whose complex flavors took over the house, I made frequent trips to the stove to observe this masterpiece. Brother Antonio, it seemed, was as full of knowledge and wisdom as his meals were full of flavor. Both the meals and the wisdom brought you back for seconds, thirds, and wonderful recollections for months and years afterward.

Was I looking for wisdom or guidance? Not that day. I was back in the mode of wandering somewhat aimlessly, wishing there were a cure to the emptiness I would feel even after accomplishing what I thought truly mattered. I had hunted down several career goals, thinking that when I had them, happiness, joy, peace, "success" would be mine. Despite climbing these ladders relatively rapidly, I hadn't found that elusive feeling that I thought should come flooding into my life upon arrival. Not only was I now in the mode of wandering, but I had added a gift of sharing my wisdom of the path to a successful life with others. Of course I brought all of this into the kitchen with Brother Antonio on that first meeting. He had studied many of the greatest minds of the human race. My interpretation of how this discussion should proceed over a bowl (okay several bowls) of what Brother Antonio informed me was a classic poor farmer's rustic Tuscan Sausage Spinach Tortellini Soup was quite simple. I figured that I would have to help the good monk unlearn much of what he thought about the world. The monk, however, was both convinced and convincing about this idea that God is intimately involved in our daily lives. Not only that, but he let me know that God will communicate with His children, including me, through any and all mediums. Am I still allowed to ignore God? Certainly. I may even be very good at it. Most of us are quite good at this. Interesting. The timing could not have been better for this friendship to begin. Each road I had taken to get to the life I thought I wanted to live was not ending in a sense of peaceful satisfaction. Instead, these roads brought me to a sense of purposelessness. I had even resorted to reading spiritual books, I suppose with a hope that perhaps centuries of spiritual wisdom just might have some answers. Was this one of the methods God was using to connect with me? I was not yet convinced, but had decided that there was little to lose from reading a few books. Something C. S. Lewis wrote about God's request to us collided with Brother Antonio's words: "Give me All. I don't want so much of your time and so much of your money and so much of your work: I want You.... the question is not what we intended ourselves to be, but what He intended us to be when He made us."

Not sure I was ready for that. Then again, when does a tremendous lesson in life come exactly when you or I say, "Timing is perfect! At this moment, I am quite ready for a lesson that will turn everything upside down!"? Does there need to be a spiritual component to this quest? Can we keep things simple by living a neatly compartmentalized life? Work goes in this box. Family in that. Spirituality over there. Political views in the fridge, second shelf on the right. Must they overlap? Couldn't one invade or interfere with the others? I was venturing into a new world, crossing through the wardrobe into Narnia, the magical land of another C.S. Lewis classic. I would find out later in my quest that Lewis was a friend of J.R. Tolkien, author of The Hobbit and The Trilogy of the Rings. Furthering my curiosity, I found that Lewis was an agnostic that converted to Christianity after many intellectually challenging conversations and wrote The Chronicles of Narnia in a competition with Tolkien over who could better depict humanity's spiritual journey through children's fiction. I had my doubts and concerns. What if the corporate world, the world in which I felt I was doing fairly well, didn't really appreciate a mixing of things not work-related? Or what if progressing on a spiritual path and building a career or business were mutually exclusive goals? Somehow, I started to see hypocrisy in these very questions. My work life had already interfered, unquestioned and unchallenged, with every other aspect of my life. This was the norm. This was life in the 21st Century. Brother Antonio, a series of books, a lot of questions, and an unsettled feeling that there must be more to life were about to collaborate and shake my world up a little more than I had bargained for.

Let me try not to get too far ahead of myself here. Isn't that a constant temptation when you've been down a path, care deeply about another person, and want to help them see where the path leads? Join me back in that kitchen eating a 5 course meal all served out of a single pot. I am lost and pretending to be full of a most profound wisdom that no one throughout thousands of years of human history had ever pieced together. That poor, patient monk. He

> **"Men occasionally stumble over the truth, but most of them pick themselves up and hurry off as if nothing ever happened."**
> ~ **Winston Churchill**

must have known how lost I was and kept on the message that God speaks to us in whichever means necessary. At the time, I believe that I may have even been proud of my most humble moment in the conversation. It came when I realized that God may use a memory, an experience, a friend, a stranger, a book, a place, or even a frying pan over the head to get your attention. In this brief moment of openness to an answer, I started reflecting on all the moments that may just have been frying pans in my life. How many had I experienced? It certainly seemed like I already had more than my share. Maybe, just maybe, I had become an expert at Winston Churchill's great line: "Men occasionally stumble over the truth, but most of them pick themselves up and hurry off as if nothing ever happened."

That first conversation left three lasting imprints on my memory. 1.) God has a plan for me and my life. 2.) He will share it with me so I might want to start paying attention. 3.) Brother Antonio makes some unbelievable Italian food. Isaac Newton once said "I was able to see so far because I have stood on the shoulders of giants." It might just be time to start looking for the right giants upon whose shoulders I should be standing. This

Who are you BECOMING?

monk would be worth getting to know and now I was starting to think that there just might be even more questions to which I did not have very good answers.

Had anyone traveled this path before? I drove home thanking God for Italian Soup and for planting a seed of thought that I promised I would nurture.

A sesame bagel and a "doctah"

There is no bread-like item in the world like a fresh baked New York water bagel – I've been fortunate to travel quite a bit and have yet to find a bagel that compares to New York's finest!

"We need a doctah in the family," Grandma Connie said, rather offhandedly as I sliced a NY sesame bagel at the dining room table of her co-op in Queens, NY. I guess it was close to my 18th birthday and that big college decision was rapidly approaching. Often when I speak to audiences, I will discuss a Greek obsession around the phrase "Know Thyself". Apparently it wasn't just something about which Socrates waxed eloquently on one spring afternoon. This expression was carved above the entrance to the Delphi Oracle, considered to be a center for wisdom by the Greeks. Centuries later, William Shakespeare declared "To thine own self be true, and it must follow, as the night the day, thou canst not then be false to any man." To thine own self be true necessitates self-knowledge. Early 21st century America may not quite share this "Know Thyself" obsession. From where do I draw this conclusion? Here is just one example of many.

Each September, across our great nation, more than two million college freshmen, aged and versed approximately 18 years within our culture, are asked to declare a major. How will you spend this life that you've been given? To which most respond, "Which major pays well but doesn't have any 8 am classes or require too much math?" This brings me full circle back to the sesame bagel. Grandma's comment caught my attention. "Doctah" – I could do that. It pays well, too. I wouldn't learn about the "no 8 am classes" condition for another few months. As I spread cream cheese on that NY sesame bagel, I wasn't really sure if I would enjoy being a "doctah" or if it would be the best use of my talents on this earth, but what does that have to do with anything? A few short months later, I'm a pre-med student loading up on bio, chemistry, math, and some elective courses in business, psychology, anthropology, and other subjects I had deemed meaningless but required. Years later I would probably have referred to this as Type 1 "Muda" in Toyota Production System speak: necessary non-value added waste, required in the current system, but not actually adding any value to the product (me). What do psychology, anthropology, philosophy have to do with a career? Why would I need that stuff to be a "doctah" or start my own practice someday? As I write this now, I wonder how I made it to 18 without yet grasping this.

Despite my tremendous self-pronounced wisdom, my mother was somehow able to convince me that an informal internship with our family doctor for a few weeks would prove worthwhile. Without completely appreciating the value of this arrangement, I agreed to tag along with Doctor Woodley, a family doctor, over the course of about 6 weeks. One afternoon, as we drove back to Doc's office after visiting several patients in two nearby hospitals, a frying pan hit me square on the top of my head. No, it was not a real frying pan. Maybe it should have been; I might have applied its lesson more quickly.

The sun was warm for mid-December. I was in the passenger seat of an older gray Saab hatchback driving through the "notch", a section of road just north of Scranton, Pennsylvania, that was carved out of bedrock alongside a small winding stream. My

> "There are two great days in a person's life – the day we are born and the day we discover why."
> ~William Barclay

mind wandered back and forth between the beautiful weather and getting back to campus for basketball practice. Doc Woodley casually mentioned that some people choose medicine as a profession because a family member thinks it's a good idea and would pay well. Unaware that he just may have been diagnosing me, I responded with the classic 18-year-old "hmmm", but I did sit a bit more upright and decided to listen more closely. His next words: "You can make money doing just about anything, but if you don't love what you do, you will not be excited to get out of bed every morning." "Yup" is my deep and thoughtful reply. "Thank you so much for saving me decades of misery" or "Brilliant!" might have been more appropriate. Either way, I had changed my major within a few weeks. The memory of that car ride and the selection of my next major are as clear as the stars over Nantucket on a cloudless night. Next major: Mechanical Engineering. Why? A book in my mother's office of career planning listed it as paying a starting salary of $31,400. Oh, we can add that math and science also came easy to me. Could this really happen outside of the twilight zone? The doctor's words are crystal clear to this day, yet I decided on my next major without thinking about what I would love to jump out of bed to do each morning. Dear Doctor Woodley, the next time you have profound wisdom to share, please bring a real frying pan with you. You may also want to engrave the lesson on the frying pan so that it stays with the recipient!

A Bigger Role

Doctor Woodley's was not the only frying pan to hit me that fateful freshman year.

Coach: _"Fanning, we need you to play a bigger role"_

_Me_ _(without really looking up from the drills I was in the middle of): "Got it, coach."_

In my mind, I tried to figure out exactly what that meant. We had been ranked # 3 in the country for Junior College basketball, but three of our stars were suddenly gone. They had "borrowed" a roommate's credit card and took several shopping sprees. Despite their loss, our team still had a tremendous amount of talent. Like most good junior college programs, we had several division one caliber players that didn't have the academics or SAT scores to get into a D1 program. "Bigger Role ... bigger role ... bigger ROLE ... BIGGER ROLE" kept repeating in my head as I worked on post moves and footwork. A college student today might not understand this concept, but this was before our smart phones could look up any phrase and bring you every possible interpretation in a Google-second. I racked my brain for several days after that challenge. What could "bigger role" translate into? Shoot more? Dribble more? Play more? Create plays more? Take it to the rack more? All of my translations involved me with the ball in my hands more. Bigger role? Count me in. I could imagine so many great storybook endings to that season. Let's try the real ending this time around. We were knocked out of the playoffs very early, losing to a team that we should have handled easily. Were we less talented than this team? No. Did they just have a great game? No. We lost as a result of one of the most overlooked lessons of today's culture. Character. Our talent and skill gave us the ability to beat just about any team. We had serious and contagious character flaws as a team. Our work ethic was inconsistent. Our humility as a team was non-existent. Our determination to win was trumped by our commitment to personal stats. Character: who are you as a person? Skill: what can you do? The ancient Greeks used the word charassein, meaning to scratch or engrave. An artisan would make his mark, or character, on a piece of pottery. Customers would come to associate the artisan's mark with the work that represented that individual. It could translate into "always creative" or "well made" or "cheap junk" or "inconsistent – sometimes amazing, sometimes sloppy." The character of the artist morphed into a symbol for who that person was. Our team's mark would have included "flashes of brilliance" and "selfish play."

> "Parents are usually more careful to bestow knowledge on their children rather than virtue."
> ~ Buckminster Fuller

What bigger role was coach asking of me? He wanted me to lead. Lead the team. Set the tone. Influence the other players towards a different set of standards. Affect the team's character. I had yet to stumble over one of the greatest questions of life, but this season provided a serious clue. Who am I BECOMING? Who am I helping those around me to BECOME? Years later, I would start to understand this simple yet profound formula:

C x S = L (Q&Q)

Character x Skill = Leadership (Quantity and Quality)
(as a leader, as a team, as a business)

Thomas Jefferson wisely quipped "There is a natural aristocracy ... the grounds of which are talent and virtue [loosely translated into skill and character]." In presenting this formula, I do realize that most models are wrong, although some are useful. Let's look at the usefulness of C x S = L.

Although our combined team skill level was close to 10 out of 10, the combined character of our team was closer to a 2 or 3. The result: the best value our team could create was a 20 or 30 out of a possible 100. This simplest of formulas sent us home from the playoffs well before we thought our season should have ended. We did not know the formula. I venture that many teams do not. Our naiveté did not stop the formula from taking its toll on that basketball season. How many sports teams fail to understand this and come to a similar fate? Families? Businesses? People? Later in the book we'll address the best approach I have ever found to build character in yourself and others.

You call that a letter of recommendation?

How many frying pans could one college freshman need? This one would be right in line with the first three. You may not be shocked by this: As a college freshman, I had already come to the realization that I had it all figured out...

In early April, my professor for an *Introduction to Engineering* course announced that our next test grade would be based on how well each student studied, learned, and applied the engineering fundamentals required for this exercise. During a class period in mid-May, we would fly paper airplanes that each of us designed and built. The cold, harsh judge would be a stopwatch, measuring the amount of time that each airplane would remain aloft. This particular freshman built a 60 second airplane in 120 seconds. This was a test grade and worth putting in that extra effort. On the day of the "performance" we met outside the classroom door and headed up the stairwell towards our launch pad: the roof of this old brick three story building. My peers arrived with these intricate designs – rubber bands, adjustable weights for balance, adjustable wings, and even books on aerodynamics. Seeing these sophisticated aircraft as I approached the classroom, I hid my folded single sheet of paper plane inside my notebook. I was just a bit embarrassed for my classmates' excessive efforts that I expected to beat with this simple one sheet plane. From the roof of that three story building, a group of aspiring future space shuttle designers began to launch aircraft. The scoring process was simple. We had the entire class period of about 50 minutes for each of us to record our highest score. Fifteen seconds in the air would be an A. Fourteen – B. Thirteen – C. Twelve – D. Eleven or less – F. Launch one was less than impressive, scoring in the eleven seconds or less category. F. Nothing to worry about. I ran quite briskly down three flights of stairs to gather my plane from the lawn. On the return trip, I remembered that there was a computer lab on the first floor, right next to the stairwell. Making a quick detour, I grabbed an extra sheet of paper from one of the printers. Plane number two might have taken 27 seconds to build, partly on the way up the next two flights of stairs. I had two aircraft for round two, but the results weren't any better. A slight gust of wind did temporarily pick up one of my planes mid-flight, but it then spiraled and I was still sitting on an F. My third trip down the steps and out onto the lawn to gather up the planes was even faster. On my return trip, I ducked into the computer lab once again, this time completely emptying two printers of all their paper. I sprinted up the stairs, carrying what must have been about 250 sheets of paper.

Launch attempt #3 with about thirty minutes left in class and somewhere around 252 sheets of paper for college-level airplane construction might go a little better. To make up for six weeks of lost planning, I was now searching for every possible angle. Ah, the ledge along the edge of the roof was about three feet high. If I stood on that, I would gain a little more potential flight time. Add to that launching with my launch hand stretched as high as I could reach and my planes would take off from about eleven

> "The heights by great men reached and kept were not attained by sudden flight, but they, while their companions slept, were toiling upward in the night."
> ~ Henry Wadsworth Longfellow

feet above the roof of the building. Let's give it a shot. First plane – some success! 12 seconds. A solid D. A D? I never had a D in anything in my life. This was not the way the day was supposed to unfold. Don't get overanxious, I thought. Still about twenty-nine minutes of flying time. Plane #2: death-spiral. I hurriedly started to build a third plane while calculating the number of planes I would have time to build. Should I build ultra-quickly, launching thirty or even sixty planes that were not very well formed? Or build two-minute planes, limiting my launches to fifteen? Before making that decision, a spark of an idea – you can refer to it as a flash of brilliance if you choose – grabbed my attention. This decision I was wrestling with was not the decision

17

at all. Making planes was an entirely useless process. My attention was captivated by that slight gust of wind from the previous round that had given my plane a boost mid-flight. What if...?

I just had to test this idea. As I stood tiptoe on the ledge, I stretched my hand to the heavens, holding a single flat sheet of printer paper and released it gently into the breeze. My new "wingless" aircraft fluttered, caught a breeze, and then fluttered downward again. Another breeze provided a slight lift and course adjustment. This new plane that required absolutely no assembly had remained aloft for 11 seconds, and without the best breeze. This would work. I just had to launch enough and get the right wind conditions. A calm came over me as I picked up the 249 remaining sheets of paper and climbed back onto the ledge. Holding the stack in one hand and launching with the other, I began to demonstrate my mastery of aerodynamics. To this day, I wonder what my classmates on that rooftop might have been thinking.

> "I went to the woods because I wished to live deliberately, to front only the essential facts of life, and see if I could not learn what it had to teach, and not, when I came to die, discover that I had not lived."
> ~ Henry David Thoreau

After about twenty or thirty "wingless, no assembly required" airplane launches, this special "got it all figured out" freshman dropped a sheet of paper that "flew" for 18 seconds (two perfect gusts of wind) and earned that A! I actually finished the class with the highest grade for the semester and, since my professor was also a business consultant – something I thought I might want to try, I asked for a letter of reference. The wise professor wrote a very brief letter of reference, which he placed in my file. This "got it all figured out" freshman was actually a bit angry with the professor for the letter of recommendation ... which read simply, "Jonathan Fanning has a lot of talent, but only does enough to get by." What was I thinking about my teacher the moment that I read the letter? Oh thank you, that's exactly what I needed to hear? I was hoping you'd write that. I actually haven't used the letter. It's still in my file.

Ralph Waldo Emerson wisely quipped, "The chief want in a person's life is for someone to help you and I become who we can be." My professor was doing just that. Did I want to hear it? Did I need to hear it?

Think about this for a few minutes. You have some people in your life who have helped you become someone that you would not have become without their influence. Think about a few of those people. How many do you have in your life? It's a small number for most of us. If one of these people who helped you become who you were capable of becoming asked for your help with something this weekend, would you respond with "let me check my calendar" or would you be there, no matter the circumstances? We need more people in our lives like this. Seek them out. We need to be this person for more people in our lives. Be that person for one more person in your life.

Don't all great teachers tend to give us what we need, but not necessarily what we want? I had a great high school basketball coach for one season. His mantra was that we would be the best conditioned team in the league. We ran more "suicide" drills or "ladders" than I care to remember. It's a drill where the whole team lines up on the line at one end of the gym, then sprint to the foul line (extended) and back, then to half court and back, then to the opposite foul line extended and back, then to the opposite out of bounds line and back. Then "Again!" If you've ever seen the movie "Miracle" about the 1980 US Hockey team, there's a tremendous scene where coach Herb Brooks has the team skating this drill again and again and again and again. Brooks' line, "The common man achieves nothing."

Great mentors help us become. Great mentors might meet us where we are, but they don't let us stay there. Great mentors... I didn't exactly call them that back then!

Allow these questions to permeate your life. Who are you BECOMING? Who are you helping those around you to BECOME?

One of life's biggest questions

Frying pans come in many shapes, sizes, metals, finishes, and weights. If you were hit in the head, in the same exact spot each time, with every imaginable frying pan, would you think that someone was trying to send you a message? Would you listen? I imagine you're saying yes. Good to hear. I ignored the coincidence for a while!

Finally I started thinking that these questions -

"Who am I BECOMING?"

"Who am I helping those around me to BECOME?"

- should be central to my life. I started thinking this. Did that change everything? Not immediately. A few more frying pans later, I thought more about putting these questions at the center of my life. A few more frying pans and I was starting to get the message, I think...

Who am I BECOMING?

Put the book down and think about this for a few minutes. A year from now, you'll be more patient. Or you won't. You'll be more courageous. Or you won't. You'll be more loving, more forgiving. Or you won't. You'll be more focused, more clear in your personal vision. Or you won't.

Who am I helping those around me to BECOME?

Let these two questions become a part of your day, part of your week, and part of your life. Then email me at JFanning@JonathanFanning.com and let me know what impact this has had on your life.

Who are you BECOMING?

Chapter 2

The "Examined" Life

Have you ever been so busy that a week, a month, a year, a decade seemed to just slip away? On Walden Pond, Henry David Thoreau wisely wrote something akin to, "It's not enough to be busy; so are the ants. What are you busy about?" (Thoreau used industrious instead of busy, but I thought poetic license might help with our discussion.) For many of us the response is simply "great question – ask me another time because I'm pretty busy today."

A large utility company hired me to speak to their leadership team. In the discussions about what value the organization needed to get from my talk, I was informed that they do not need to hear "take time to reflect" because "we don't have time for that." Wow. That

> "The unexamined life is not worth living"
> ~ Socrates

got me thinking. I hate to admit it, but my mind left the meeting for a few minutes after that statement. From a technology perspective, we live in an amazing moment of productivity. Yet with all this technology, have we become so caught up in the tyranny of routine, of doing, doing, doing that we cannot spare a moment to look at just what it is that we are doing? What if everyone in your family bought into that mindset? Wouldn't yesterday, today, and tomorrow blend together? As a parent of two amazing little girls, I am often inspired with my daughters' ability to step back from their approach, evaluate it, modify it, and try again. When our youngest, Maya, was just two-and-a-half years old, one of her favorite games was Puppy Kittens, which she and I played together on my bed. It's an amazing game. She is a tiny puppy and I am a kitten. Then we switch. Then Maya throws one of her almost-three-year-old curveballs, "I a tiny puppy and you a big puppy! Sleep time. Cock-a-doodle Doooooo! Wake up time."

Since I do some of my work from home, there are times when daddy is not ready to play Puppy Kittens. Does this deter Maya? Not the first time. "Dadda, you want to play Puppy Kitten?" Not the second time. "Dadda, come with Maya." Not the third time. Taking my hand, locking eyes and magically creating a sparkle in her own eyes, "Dadda, you can be the big puppy!" Will she try the same approach several times? Sure. Might she resort to crying? Perhaps. I'll not make a claim for a perfect family! One thing Maya will not do? Throw in the towel without examining her approach. At two and a half, Maya understood corporate America's decades of excitement over Six Sigma. Set up a few experiments and find out what creates the result you seek. Brilliant. Have we really become too busy to step back and evaluate our experiences? My thoughts returned to the meeting quite rapidly when I realized that I was just as guilty of not examining life as the next person. Only now I was examining my world while I was supposed to be examining theirs. Welcome back to the meeting, Jonathan.

Now it's your turn. When do you examine what you're doing, how you're doing it, and how well it's working? And yes, this would apply to everything. I walked out of that meeting asking myself how often I use the Too Busy card to avoid changing an approach. A friend had once told me "most people lead complicated lives to avoid changing them." That saying came back to me as I started my car after meeting with the utility company. Which parts of my life were intentionally complicated?

24

In one of my businesses, I had evaluated the marketing processes with an almost obsessive approach so we knew which levers created results. Now these marketing processes were in place and I hadn't stopped to reflect on their effectiveness in a while because we were busy with other things. Many follow a similar pattern when dating a future spouse: we reflect on what phrases get their attention, what appetizers they will enjoy, what movies will have them walking on air, what trips might be amazing memories. Then we are married. Reflecting on what matters most might just get steamrolled by our busy-ness.

Socrates was on trial for corrupting the youth of Athens, encouraging them to think for themselves and challenge the assumptions of the then modern world. His persecutors gave him options: he could have a life in prison, be exiled, or choose the death penalty. Socrates' response, "The unexamined life is not worth living." It's very difficult to imagine being on trial for encouraging students to think. But today's modern culture seems to encourage a lack of life examination in its own way. There may not be a death penalty for thinking, but I see many parents car pooling their children from one event to the next, keeping busy, leading complicated lives. Do most of us lead complicated and busy lives to avoid examining and, perhaps, changing them? At various times, I have complicated my life with some or all of the following:

- Start three businesses, almost simultaneously
- Volunteer for more community projects than I had time for
- Try to visit every family member on every holiday
- Fit 10 activities into a Saturday

- Want a seminar, training event, or marketing program to follow my precise plan
- Vacation with a plan for every single day
- Work out, read, prep for next day's meetings, watch some NBA basketball playoffs - all in 3 hrs
- Play with kids, talk with my wife about finances, plans for weekend, work on my business's hiring process
- Write this book with Maya climbing on my lap and Ella climbing on my head
- Change the world, be home for dinner every night, attend every child's big events, find the best deals in the grocery store, find great tenants for my 4 unit apartment building

Is there no solution to this madness? What frying pan do I need to make a change? One word. Simplicity.

Simplicity. A few years ago I watched a movie about Saint Francis of Assisi entitled "Brother Sun, Sister Moon." In one scene, Francis and his group are rebuilding a stone church joyfully. They begin to sing:

> "If you want to build your dreams, take your time go slowly.
> Do few things but do them well, simplicity is holy."

That was one beautiful, soft, and much-needed frying pan telling me SIMPLIFY.

Examine your life. Where do you need to simplify so that you have time to examine your life? Today is a great day to take one complication out of your busy life. Maybe you can just pick one complication from this list:

- Shut off your phone for an hour each day.
- Shut off your phone for two hours each day.
- Shut off your phone for fifteen minutes each day.

Shall I continue? That's a tough one for most of us. It invades our quiet time. Invades our breakfast time, lunch time, family dinner, conversations, and life!

- Watch one less TV program each week.
- Pause for 1 full second before responding to questions or before adding your advice
- Watch one less sporting event each week.
- Drive for five minutes without the radio on each day.
- Ask a friend how they've been and then take a temporary vow of silence and let them fill you in.
- Make completely home-made pancakes on a Saturday morning.
- Camp in a tent for a weekend.
- Shut off all entertainment for a day except books.
- Say no to one project.
- Block off a day (or at least several hours) each week and dedicate it to building relationships. Don't allow work to seep into that block of time.

Socrates gave his life so the citizens of Athens, you, and I would hear this lesson.

Please hear it.

They *lied* on their resumes?

After hiring hundreds of people, I have come to this astounding realization: resumes may be one of the greatest cover-ups of our modern world.

To intentionally falsify a resume is one thing. Perhaps that is also common. What I refer to here, though, is completely unintentional. The process looks something like this:

I read a resume. Note candidate's 12 years' experience as a supervisor, working with children. Anticipate interviewing highly qualified and skilled candidate. Reality: Meet and find that candidate has only 1 years' experience repeated 12 times.

Whatever habits, techniques, approaches they used in year one have now become thoroughly ingrained in their days. If a child doesn't listen 3 consecutive times, the teacher resorts to a threat or raises her voice, or may have some other solution, better or worse. Regardless of the effectiveness of the solution, this "12 year" candidate has become very consistent at their year one approach.

By the age of 25, I was advising corporate leaders that were, on average, more than twice my age. Most of my career (just 3 years at that point) had been in manufacturing companies. I was teaching leaders with 30 years' experience how to change their leadership and the direction of their organizations. People would often tell me that I must be older than I looked. Not the case. How do you get more out of a few years than the rest of the world? Create a feedback loop. As I once heard leadership and sales expert Brian Tracy say, "learn more, try more, learn more, try more, learn more, try more." In this realm, I was truly starting to see that the

> "A man is his own easiest dupe, for what he wishes to be true he generally believes to be true"
> ~ Demosthenes

formula introduced earlier (Character x Skill = Quality and Quantity of Leadership) really holds true. I call the trait that goes with this chapter "Applied Teach-ability", or the ability to both learn and apply lessons. I put the two words together because the field of leadership development is full of people who know but don't know. "You don't know what you don't know and that's why you don't do. Because to know and not to do is not to know."

Jonathan's guide to applied teach-ability: fail early and often, but not repeatedly. Let me share an example. A few years ago, I had the chance to attend a three day real estate investment seminar with about 40 people. The speaker was full of great tips on finding properties, negotiating price and terms, tenant screening, affecting your credit score, analysis, and much more. One tip was to keep in touch with the group so we could help each other out. I liked that and we passed around a list to get phone numbers and emails of each attendee. Within a year, I had purchased a four unit rental property. A year into owning the building, I decided to contact all of the participants to see how their investments were progressing. Not a single person of the dozens that I was able to contact had purchased a property. It was now about two years after the seminar. What lessons could these participants have learned from the program?

A colleague of mine on one project brought up the idea of guiding senior management in a Fortune 20 company to read and discuss Dale Carnegie's classic, *How to Win Friends and Influence People*. I have to admit, I was a little hesitant about the idea of a "book club" for senior executives at one of the world's largest and most recognized companies. At the first meeting, one executive summarized the first section of this people skills classic in a sentence, "Don't criticize, condemn, or complain... what can we talk about?" This organization's culture was built around those three words. Reading a few chapters from an almost century old book helped the leadership team to start reflecting. It seems that most of us don't take a look at how we operate until something triggers it.

Looking in the mirror is only part of the process of applied teach-ability. Holding up an image to the mirror and then doing something to bring us closer to the image we have decided to pursue is the rest of the process. Without a feedback loop, without "applied teach-ability, "Who am I BECOMING?" decays into "Who was I and am I still!"

Ben, George, Socrates and the foundation for the "Who are you BECOMING?" plan

Applied Teach-ability must be something new, a concept I've created. Sure. I was studying all aspects of business when I came across an old book called *How I Raised Myself from Failure to Success in Selling* (written by Frank Bettger in 1947). Bettger built a tremendous career in sales by creating his own version of Ben Franklin's 13 Week Plan for Virtuous Living. The program is quite simple, yet unbelievably effective. The simplicity of it had me fooled for a while. Maybe you are under the same impression I have lived under: things must be complicated to be any good.

Before I get into the plan, I want to explore this "complication = effective" myth. For several years, I had been building the most successful franchise in a children's fitness network. We offered fitness programs at daycares and birthday parties for young children. My top marketing approaches:

1. Deliver great experiences, creating referrals!

2. Provide free events for organizations that already have
   hundreds of young children attending and see #1
   above.

Both are extremely simple yet extremely effective. A local preschool that I have worked with will serve as our example for hiring, training, retaining great employees. The director has been with the preschool for over 3 decades. She offhandedly mentioned to me that she is a bit worried about staff recently. When I inquired further, she explained her secret to getting a great staff: hire parents of children who went to your school only after you have seen them with children for several years. No surprises. You know who they are, how dependable they are, how they interact with children in many varied scenarios. Simple. Highly effective.

A final example in the art of giving people feedback: aggressive love and humble truth. I could list 21 rules for effective feedback, the 7 keys to telling someone what they need to hear, 10 tips to ensure your feedback is heard, the 4 part model for… OR we can try the five word model in the first sentence of this paragraph. Aggressive Love and Humble Truth. Aggressively value the person with whom you are sharing feedback. Then, with personal humility, share the truth of a message that person needs to hear. Simple. Highly effective.

The plan that follows is also simple and highly effective.

At the age of twenty, Ben Franklin created a plan that will radically change your life, your business, your family, your community, the whole world around you – if you are ready for it. On a boat trip to Europe, Franklin outlined 12 virtues around which he would build his character. After he returned to the colonies, Franklin shared his plan with a Quaker friend, who pointed out that young Ben was thought proud, overbearing, and rather insolent. According to his own autobiography, Franklin then argued with the friend. I could just picture a prideful young Franklin saying, "Proud? Me? I think not!" As a result, a thirteenth virtue, Humility, was added to young Ben's plan.

As a printer, Franklin built a score sheet to track his progress in developing these virtues. Each week, he would put his primary focus on just one virtue, scoring himself on his score sheet daily, thus creating the examined life. Two questions he added to his journal: start the day with "What good will I do today?" and conclude the day with "What good have I done today?" Hold the result you wish to pursue to the mirror, evaluate, and make modifications. Franklin would go through his 13 Week Plan for Virtuous Living in the order of his 13 virtues, one per week, and then repeat the process. Each year, the plan would be repeated 4 times. In his autobiography,

> **"There is nothing new under the sun."**
> **~ Ecclesiastes**

Franklin explains the plan, shares his score sheet, and notes that while he may not have mastered humility, none heard him utter a dogmatic expression over the last 50 years of his life. Instead, he would offer opinions with introductory phrases such as "I may be wrong, I often am, but perhaps we might consider..." and "It so appears to me at present ..." This intense focus on developing virtue brought the young prideful, overbearing, and insolent Benjamin Franklin the degree of humility and diplomacy required for his role in founding a nation and as an ambassador, asking France for financial and military assistance. By the time of the First Continental Congress, Franklin had been practicing his plan for almost 50 years. Four weeks of each year had been dedicated to the development of humility, with a feedback loop each day, compounded over those 50 years. Reflecting on that, I had to ask myself how many weeks I have dedicated to developing humility, or any other trait, with that amount of intentionality.

After stumbling upon this approach, I did what most people would do; nod, think to myself "now that's a great plan", and carry on with my life as usual. Revisiting the plan some time later, I thought it was just too good to ignore. Of course this time around, I spent a considerable amount of time trying to arrive at my own 13 character traits or virtues before getting started with any real work. After this unintentional stalling process of trying to settle on 13 virtues, I finally decided that I would just get started with some plan. I picked a few virtues and started running through a four week plan. When I finished week four, I started over with week one. A few months into this process, I eliminated one of my original virtues, but continued the plan. Over time, I have modified the plan several times and I will outline a process that I trust will add tremendous value to your life in the next section.

The Framework

Before sharing the process to building your own "Who am I BECOMING?" plan, I think it necessary to fill you in on a little challenge I have struggled with in the leadership development world. Through a decade or more of trying to help leaders become better leaders, I have read and re-read hundreds of books about heroes, leaders, legends, world class companies, championship sports teams, hall of fame athletes, social activists, political leaders, spiritual leaders, etc. At first, I was caught up in the "if it's published, it must be true" fallacy. Apparently, we have a tendency to believe that which is written at a rather high confidence level. The internet has certainly taken us for a ride on that tendency. Under this assumption that the experts, authors, CEO's, coaches all had the right recipe, I tried to decipher exactly which traits were most important to develop. Then the illusion fell apart. It was subtle at first, but then became one big mess in a hurry. Stephen Covey had taught me to think Win-Win. Donald Trump promoted win-lose with two questions: who wins and how much? Book after book promotes 21 laws, 9 rules, 7 habits, 14 steps, 5 traits, 101 secrets, 50 keys, and on and on and on.

Although I had finally realized that philosophy, psychology, anthropology, communication, and English might have some value in the journey to running the whole ship, or any ship, for that matter, I had not abandoned math entirely. I added up these rules, laws, and habits, arriving at a very large number. In order to lead or succeed, one must be no

> "If I have seen a little further it is by standing on the shoulders of giants."
> ~ Isaac Newton

more than a point or two below perfect, in every way. Patient, firm, kind, assertive, forgiving, courageous, a tremendous listener, a gifted orator, able to walk on or above water, regardless of salt content.

Can they all be right? Are they all wrong? Are some right some of the time? Are they all just blowing smoke? These are the questions I started asking. The conclusion requires a brief aside.

Please travel to Rome with me for clarification, figuratively for now! The Pantheon holds the Guinness record for being the world's largest concrete dome without any internal reinforcements. It is quite an impressive building. The tomb of Raphael (the artist, not my little brother's one time favorite Ninja Turtle) is inside. As you enter, the vastness of the open space gives a sense of awe. Compounding the effect is a shaft of sunlight allowed entrance through the 30 foot diameter oculus (circular hole) in the middle of the domed ceiling. Yes, when it rains, the rain comes right through that 30 foot hole. The structure is a marvel that was originally built in 27 B.C., just over 2,000 years ago, and then rebuilt about 1,900 years ago. How does it stand with no internal supports? Part of the secret: 8 barrel vaults, or very dense pillars, are built into the walls. These pillars are 21 feet thick and made of the most dense stone and concrete to be found. The 8 pillars hold the weight of the structure. This impressive structure withstands the test of time and amazes visitors still today.

8 Pillars.

Here is the point: leadership, a tremendous life, a great athletic career, an amazing family, a world-class business or non-profit organization – they can be built on a number of pillars. Do some matter more than others? Absolutely. The question is, what pillars are you intentionally building? And how are you doing with that?

My experience has been that most of us haven't even decided on the pillars, let alone create a plan to strengthen them. After several years of intense study, teaching this process to thousands of people, and using versions of the plan myself, I have arrived at a process for you to create your very own "Who am I BECOMING?" plan.

Get started today. This plan is too simple and too powerful to wait.

Who am I BECOMING plan:

Step 1: Select 3 virtues or character traits that you want to solidify in your life. You can add more or re-evaluate the traits in the future, but for now, select 3 that you will start with TODAY.

Step 2: Rotate through these 3 traits, with a full week's focus on each and then repeat.

Step 3: Examine your days   Daily, ask yourself these questions, with your focus on that week's pillar:
What will I do today?
How did it work?

(Visit us online at www.JonathanFanning.com for tools to help with this process.)

Step 4: Find a partner to go through the process with you. Review progress weekly.   This may be a co-worker, family member, friend, mentor, coach, or spiritual adviser.

Step 5: Over time, you may wish to add or remove a trait, or even change the time frame.

An important consideration for implementing this plan is a lesson borrowed from coaching baseball in Tuscany and Will Smith in the movie, *The Legend of Bagger Vance*. Will Smith's character is coaching Matt Damon's character, Bagger Vance, on his golf swing. At one point, Will Smith says, "You've got to find your authentic swing, Mr. Vance, you've got to find your authentic swing." He's telling the golfer that there is a framework to swinging a golf club. Within that framework is each golfer's authentic swing, the swing that works with his or her biology, psychology, and experience. In my experience helping a great friend, Steve, who played professional baseball in Arezzo, Italy, I found the same lesson. There is a framework to swinging a bat or throwing a baseball. Within that framework is each athlete's authentic swing. Italian lesson for the day:

Carica = "load"

Esplodi = "explode"

Coach Steve and I would drill the aspiring Mike Piazza's "carica ... esplodi!" Load... explode. When the pitch is delivered, a hitter needs to shift weight back and then explode the bat and body towards the ball. How each hitter times this can vary significantly. Part of the framework is to load and explode. Each hitter's authentic swing is their way within the way. Different bodies, different minds, different psychologies. Load... explode. Find your authentic swing.

Developing virtue, character traits, and your leadership follows the same logic. There is a framework, including focus and feedback. Within that framework is your authentic swing. Perhaps 7 traits works best for you. Perhaps 2. Perhaps having a partner focusing on the same traits helps your journey. Perhaps including your boss and / or direct reports in the process will help (or hinder) your progress. Get started today. Examine your progress daily. You'll uncover that authentic swing. You'll start rapidly becoming who you are capable of becoming. Those who know you best will be astounded. I have included a tool to help you track your progress with a few sample scenarios online at www.JonathanFanning.com. Use the feedback tool every day, including scoring your day, what worked well and not so well, and what you'll try tomorrow to be more effective. Work through the process with a friend. Include your family. Allow me to share some of my experience of involving children in this journey.

Ella just turned seven years old. She is such an amazing little girl! She reminds me regularly what matters in life and that you can dream, imagine, laugh, cry, smile, love, forgive... So many moments from her life will be cherished memories forever. I think parenting is one of the most important leadership roles in all of history. We all want amazing things for our children. In speaking with so many parents, it seems that all parents want to develop tremendous character traits in their children. Unfortunately, very rarely do I meet a parent with a specific plan that is working well to accomplish this. Well, I decided to test this whole "Who are you BECOMING?" plan with my little girl, Ella, over the past many months. Keeping the authentic swing concept has helped this process more than I can describe. Through this experiment, which will absolutely continue and improve, I have learned more about this plan from Ella than I learned from Ben Franklin. Maybe Ella will invent the 21st century version of the bifocals and Franklin stove?

I started the process with the best of intentions and a solid plan. Suffice to say that I must have needed another frying pan moment. Ella efficiently taught me that she needed to buy in to the plan if it were ever going to work. Dadda, Dadda, Dadda! How many times must you learn that people must buy in to the vision before we get started with your plan? My wonderful Ella, many future clients owe you a debt of gratitude for finally getting that message through to your father. My original plan: Daddy selects the focus weeks and we get started. Ella's modification:

she selects ONE focus day that she likes and we get started. One day at a time. Maybe she didn't want to start with a 5 week program that would be repeated every single day for the rest of her life. Interesting. Maybe other human beings operate from a similar perspective. We should explore that, but another time.

Be brave, be daring!   That was our first day's focus. We talked about it the night before while reading our bedtime story. On THE day, day 1, the beginning of the rest of Ella's life, we ate breakfast and talked about being brave. What might it look like today? In school, how could Ella be brave – what actions would the daring Ella take that she might ordinarily avoid? After school, we casually discussed it: "were you brave today? Tell me about it!" At dinner, the conversation continued. What would be a way to be brave at dinner? I could try foods that I don't usually try. Mamma would be really proud of me, wouldn't you, Mamma? Were you brave today, Dadda?   How do you like that for accountability? On day 1 of project "Who is Ella BECOMING?" Ella reinforced the authentic swing concept. Making the trait part of the day's conversation, working with a friend or family member, making it fun, talking about what you could do the next time or the next day all worked within the framework. Focus and feedback. With Ella, we didn't start with a whole week focused on that trait. We made it 1 great day. We didn't need to start a new daily meeting or a program of the month. We simply talked about being brave, focused on ways to be brave, and had a little informal feedback on how being brave worked throughout the day. Focus and feedback. One day at a time.

A few days later we had another focus day. Day 2 was built around "Ella's in charge of Ella." Be responsible. Be pro-active. Choose your response. Happen to the world rather than letting the world happen to you. Ella has two favorite books which I highly recommend to every parent on the planet. We made these books part of the Christmas presents and birthday presents for every child in our lives. The Seven Habits of Happy Kids (Sean Covey, the son of Stephen Covey from 7 Habits renown) and Why am I Here? (Matthew Kelly). I am constantly on the lookout for children's books, songs, and stories that help children focus on or answer the question "Who am I BECOMING?" Why am I Here? is a short story about Max trying to figure out why he's alive. His grandfather helps him understand that he is here to become the best-version-of-himself. Max then uses that phrase to answer so many questions, including what to eat, whether he should do his homework or not, and how to treat his classmates. The first chapter of Covey's children's book is about Sammy the Squirrel being "Bored Bored Bored". Ella always requests that I read it in Sammy's voice. Just in case you may be unaware, Sammy speaks with two very different voices. He has an angry, impatient, defeatist voice when he is bored. The voice changes to one of optimism, excitement, and fun when he realizes that Sammy is in charge of Sammy and, as a result of this realization, he is capable of creating his own fun. Sammy keeps asking other people to cure his boredom by finding fun things for him to do. They each offer their ideas of fun activities and defeatist Sammy keeps emphasizing, "can't you find something fun for ME to do?" Since you are likely asking the question, the answer is yes, there is a face and posture that go with Sammy as he marches away, becoming more and more frustrated that no one is curing his boredom. When Ella – I mean Sammy - finally realizes that he is in charge of his own emotional state, he immediately finds something fun to do. You can imagine the mileage we get out of that chapter! That is one of Ella's favorite focuses now. Ella is in charge of Ella. Who gets to decide how Ella feels... what Ella thinks... how Ella behaves...?

Two traits identified! We were really making progress. Each night at bedtime, we would talk about how Ella did with Being Brave or Being in Charge of Ella. Time to add another trait. I wanted to incorporate Vision into the mix, but how? Authentic Swing. Applied Teach-ability. Learn more, try more. I sometimes share an acronym from Tom Peters in my "BECOMING a Creative Leader" seminars. WTTMTTFW. Most audiences struggle trying to figure out what the acronym stands for. Typically only one out of a few hundred will look it up. Intriguing because we have usually just covered the creative concept of looking everywhere for ideas, fighting our subtle and highly effective cultural training that there's only one answer to every question, it's in the back of the book, and if you look, you are cheating. The audience laughs at this and we talk about borrowing ideas from every source. Then I show the acronym and no one cheats. WTTMTTFW. Whoever Tries The Most Things The Fastest Wins. Not a true statement for every part of life. However, in the creative phase – in the finding what might work for your authentic swing phase – it can be invaluable. Try something. Get in motion. A friend of mine likes to say "God can't steer a parked car." Well, that's certainly incorrect, I think God could move a parked car quite easily, but the visual makes the point. WTTMTTFW. Let's get started trying approaches that might help Ella focus on clarity of vision. We started with a discussion about all the things that Ella wanted to do that weekend, which I jotted down on a blank sheet of paper. Then Ella drew a picture of each one and we tried to number them, answering the question: if I can only do one of these, which one would I choose. Great! After that worked fairly well, we expanded the process to this week or this year. That part of the plan with a 6-year-old is still under construction, but it feels like we are off to a pretty good start.

One of Ella's greatest lessons to me in this process has been allowing her to have some ability to pick the focus. She will often say, "Dadda, let's do the 'Be Brave, Be Daring' again!" As I write this, we are up to 2 or 3 focus days most weeks. A few weekends ago, Ella informed me on a Friday night that the next day would be a "Brave and Daring" day. Then she proceeded to explain a list of things she'd do that would require bravery. At bedtime, Ella interrupted story time to let me know that we could do "Be Brave, Be Daring" again on Sunday. I asked if we could make it a "Be Loving and Kind" day. Ella's enthusiastic reply: "we can do both, Dadda!" During a recent week that had me on the road speaking all week, Ella let me know that Mama had made the whole week a "Be Loving and Kind" week. Mama felt that we have been doing great with building courage and it was time to get more focus and feedback on the next quality.

Imagine...
Could your school or company do this?

Can you imagine if 10 families in your child's preschool, fourth grade class, high school, or college started this process with their families? What if an entire grade level went through the process together? Maybe the group starts with 4 traits and repeats the process monthly, involving the families and incorporating books, activities, and exercises to help with the focus. What if a whole school district, town, non-profit, charity, or company got on board? So many companies today have their core values listed on their website, displayed in their marketing literature, and painted on their walls.

Unfortunately, it often reminds me of what I refer to as the diet soda life cycle: new name, big advertising campaign to convince the world that it tastes great, the world tastes it and realizes the advertising hype was an empty promise, repeat process. Many companies have followed the identical path: created a list of values, who we are and what we stand for as a company – name the values, internal and often external advertising campaign to let the employees and customers know who we are and what we stand for, employees work in the company and customers experience the product or service, quickly realizing the advertising hype was an empty promise, repeat process. Maybe this isn't

> "Never doubt that a small group of thoughtful, committed citizens can change the world; indeed, it's the only thing that ever has."
> ~ Margaret Mead

true where you work, but I have witnessed it, even helped to create parts of the cycle across our great corporate landscape. A week before writing this chapter I visited the world headquarters of a massive company and, before a talk, noticed 5 Pillars branded to the wall. One of the pillars essentially said that you can have an opinion here, you can try things. The pillars model and explanation looked great, so I asked a member of the leadership team about them. The response went like this:

"Those?   {Long Pause - with a far off look as if remembering the scientific name for a frog}

Ahhh yes.   The 5 Pillars.   They're all important to the founders of the company.   Do you remember when they rolled that out, Sharon?   {Pause, waiting for an answer that would not come.}

Hmmm. Yeah..." {Change topic}

If this were the only incident of its kind, I might just dismiss it as an outlier. That's not even close to the case. In my work with companies large and small, I have seen a variation of the pillars in most organizations. But why are the companies that actually live by their own pillars so rare? Let's revisit the framework. Focus and feedback. It translates quite nicely into know where you are going and know where you are, evaluating progress and steering along the way. Could an authentic swing for a company be so simple as to turn the 5 pillars into a 5 week plan? I tried just that a few years ago and then turned the pillars into components of my Entrepreneur Adventure programs. Brilliant! Who am I to argue with you? Kidding. Simple and Highly Effective – yes. We'll discuss more of that in a later chapter.

A number of years ago I read an article about a Thomas Jefferson Institute study that grabbed my attention. The study was conducted as an attempt to solve a puzzle of American leadership. About 250 years ago, 13 little colonies had about 3 million inhabitants. From those 3 million, sprung hundreds of world class leaders, leaders who would shape the course and structure of civilization. Today, the population of our nation has grown to be about 100 times that size, roughly 300 million. The question posed by this study: where are the tens of thousands of world class leaders today? The Thomas Jefferson Institute analyzed the changes in our American culture over that 250 year span to figure out why the number of world class leaders as a percentage of the total population had been so dramatically reduced. Their conclusion was as simple as it was profound. Educational priorities have experienced a major evolution. 250

years ago, the primary focus of education (95 % of education, according to the study) was on character development (work ethic, honesty, humility, responsibility, courage). This study concludes that our modern American culture shows very little or no evidence of a focus on character development. Education of our future leaders has evolved, primarily over the last 150 years, slowly at first and then quite rapidly. Morals were extracted from the process. Why? Many articles and doctoral dissertations address the why. We became afraid that these morals came from religion. Instead of looking at the individual character traits, much of our culture just shunned moral development out of fear. Upon which morals could we possibly agree? Let's try to step back from this emotionally heated topic just for a moment. Take a few deep breaths with me, please. George Washington's once famous list of 110 Rules of Civility has no place in our modern world. Or does it? Look it up and see if you like some of his rules.

If you are interested in creating a fairly intense discussion, share the idea of morals and character development in schools with a group of people and watch where the conversation goes. Many have told me that character development belongs in the home, not in education. In addition, who would get to decide the character traits that my children should be taught? That, my friends, is just the start of the discussion. The time out in a sporting event should be transferred to more of our "adult" conversations.

Time Out!

What character traits shall we teach? Couldn't we at least agree on a few? Perhaps Humility would make the list? Courage? Patience? Loving? Work ethic? I think we might just agree on a lot more than we think. It is really not all that different from the corporate "5 Pillars" example above. Many of our schools already have mission and value statements created. Why not just create a simple "Who are you BECOMING?" plan with weekly focus and feedback around what we've already put into our self-created diet soda cycles? Let's take one of Abe Lincoln's greatest lessons to heart here: "Character is like a tree and reputation like its shadow. The shadow is what we think of it; the tree is the real thing." Isn't it about time our whole culture starting building on the real thing? What if you and I start with our own families today and built a simple, yet highly effective plan for making character important again? What if we build it within the framework of focus and feedback?

What would the real Patch Adams say about that?

When he told us he was Patch Adams, I understood immediately. He does work like the Robin Williams character in the movie, Patch Adams. I all but interrupted the other gentleman when he excitedly asked how people respond to him since the movie came out. I was about to make the correction that our Patch wasn't the real Patch, just that he does work like the real Patch. Besides, he looked nothing like Robin Williams. Before I put both feet into my mouth, Patch Adams let us know that the movie had certainly helped with awareness for the cause and that donations come a lot more readily now. What? The Patch Adams was really sitting next to me at, of all places, a swim up bar in a very nice all-inclusive resort on the west coast of Costa Rica! We had a four hour conversation after this realization that I will never forget. The story begins the night before, when I noticed this rather interestingly attired man at one of the cafés on the property. Everything about his appearance screamed different. Not in a good way, not in a bad way, not in a please notice me way - just quite different. His pony tail was long and purple. That mustache, also long, curled up at the ends like something out of an old western film. The eyeglasses: square, tortoise shell patterns, but not with colors you often see on adults. And a fork in his ear, well a pretty substantial dangling fork earring that would be.

I had to introduce myself to this individual, so I did. His first response, "I feel a little out of place here." Really? Any single piece of his description might have caught my attention, but the purple silk pajama-like outfit with butterflies from head to toe was the icing to top off the cake. We didn't converse much that night because the café was relatively loud, but I was thrilled to see him sitting at the swim up bar in one of

> "It's humiliating that a person who kicks a ball makes more money than a school teacher."
> ~ Patch Adams

the resort's pools the next day. That is where our four hour conversation took place. One of the most memorable parts of our conversation was Mr. Adams' take on a then recent commercial. Basketball star, Charles Barkley starts the Nike commercial saying, "I am not a role model. I am not paid to be a role model. I am paid to wreak havoc on the basketball court." Patch Adams' feelings on the issue followed the simple, yet highly effective model. We should each live our lives as a role model for others. If you are highly visible to the public, you absolutely are a role model to more people than you may be comfortable with, whether you agree or not and whether you should be or not. Fame compounds the reasons for you to build the tree. Patch Adams and President Lincoln might just agree there. What about you?

Chapter 3

Clarity

What's this life really all about?

100 years from today, what ripple effect will your life have created? Both of my grandparents on my mother's side passed away within a short time of each other. I had never liked attending wakes or funerals. That awkward, uneasy feeling would leave me without the right words or the ability to really console the grievers. Oma's and Opa's funerals started the same, but then changed this perspective entirely. Oma and Opa are the German words for grandma and grandpa, which all of us grandchildren used. Of course, we all attended. Cousins came from near and far. Even the cousins who had moved to Maine and decided that running water and electricity were not requirements in a house made the trip to Astoria, NY, for the funerals.

My Opa was one of the most patient and kind people you can imagine. All five of his children miss him deeply. I walked up to Opa's casket and thought about his life, his peaceful nature, his dependable and loyal character. Every Christmas, every Easter, every Thanksgiving he would have the house ready for all of us. We would arrive to see him grinding the potatoes to make his amazing German traditional potato dumplings, which would be devoured from our plates at each holiday dinner. "Na ya" would be his comment to the traffic en route to his house, the heavy rains, the snow, the sunshine, the heat... It was Opa's personal quasi-German phrase interpreted by us as "Okay", "Hmmm", "Yes", "Oh", "Akuna Matada". Not much rattled Opa. In fact, I can't say that I ever saw him rattled. That is not to say that we got away with things. We most definitely knew if and when Opa was disappointed in our behavior and we had no intentions of letting that happen. So many memories flooded through my mind as I knelt by the casket. Would he be proud of the way his kids and grandkids were carrying on his legacy? How can I share him with my own children and grandchildren some day? Can I make his nature, like his biology, a part of me?

Just over a year later, we gathered again for Oma's funeral. They had been married for over 60 years. In a culture where silver and bronze wedding anniversaries seem to be a dying breed, how on earth did they do it? (Who even knows how many years constitute a silver or bronze anniversary these days?) Maybe we should teach newlyweds Opa's "Naya" expression. Oma had suffered from Alzheimer's for several years prior to her death, so we really felt as if she had passed away well before this day. What a testament to Opa, thinking back on the way he cared for her even when she had no idea who he was. At times, she would hit him and push him away as he tried to feed or clean or comfort her. Early in Oma's battle with Alzheimer's, she would regularly pack for a trip back to her home town in Germany. What did she pack? Anything and everything. In plastic shopping bags. Clothes, spices, car keys, wallets, sewing materials, a shoe or two – all would go into plastic bags for the trip. Where are the car keys, Schatze (Opa's affectionate German word for sweetheart)? Years. This would go on for years. Over and over. Over a decade of this and my Opa kept an amazing patience. Once again, I knelt by the coffin of one of my mother's parents. Once again, I felt a rush of happy memories of the way they brought the family together, a steady dependable family tradition to count on even as childhood had seemed to vanish somehow suddenly.

I walked back to the unofficial "cousin" area in deep thought, only to be jolted out of it as the city cousins were teasing our Maine cousins, letting them know that we had all previously agreed on their official disassociation from the family for not having running water or electricity.

Despite the classic funeral uneasiness, Oma and Opa's funerals both brought just about every conversation back to a few words, phrases, maybe two or three sentences. "Oma was such a hard worker. So strong." "Opa was the most patient and kind person I think I've ever met." "They cared so deeply for each other." Just a few sentences. Different versions, but each time the same themes. Summing up a life. Great sentences. Great lives. Great examples. I couldn't help but start to

> "Ever more people today have the means to live, but no meaning to live for."
> ~ Viktor Frankl

ask myself, "Is that how our lives are summed up? Do we each get just a few sentences?" Somehow, through hearing and reflecting on these sentences, Oma's and Opa's funerals changed the way I looked at funerals. The emotions are still there, perhaps more powerful than in the past. Now, however, funerals are a celebration and a tribute to who a person was and what they stood for. Not long after these funerals, I even found myself walking through a cemetery and pondering which few sentences may have been shared about the strangers' graves as I slowly walked by. Someday I'll be in my own grave. What will be my few sentences? This question, my Oma and Opa's character, was bringing me back to the bigger questions that seem to get lost in our complicated culture. Too many things to get done today to spend any time on big questions. Oh, perhaps! But my sentences are being written. My few sentences. I used to think a day or two could get away from you. Now I was starting to think that a year or two can so easily slip by without asking any big questions. Thank you, Oma and Opa, for your great answers to these big questions. As I reflected on my generation's descriptions of Oma and Opa, my imagination brought me forward a few decades. How would my kids and my grandkids describe Oma and Opa, whom they had never met? Oma and Opa, your example and your lives brought me to this: "One hundred years from today, what ripple effect will your live have had?"

Know Thyself: putting big questions in order.

Who am I? What do I stand for? As a result, what should I do with my life? Those three questions in that order set the tone for the Entrepreneur Adventure immersion programs that I started a few years ago. The idea seemed simple at the beginning. I wished that young people could really experience business start-up and ownership, the ups and downs, emotions, psychology, mindset — the realities of hatching your dream and taking 100% responsibility for turning it into reality. Not only had I experienced it, but I had met too many adults with empty eyes, who had let their dreams die a slow death. I wanted to do something about this. What if I could find a way to immerse young people in the entrepreneur's journey through an intense experiential program that would change the way they saw themselves and the world around them, challenging limits, constraints, and self-imposed restrictions. Sure, Jonathan, the idea sounds simple enough. At this point, the sane reader may be asking what happened to that discussion about simplicity earlier in the book! There seem to be many clichés that guide our lives, sometimes these clichés guide us so subtly that we may not even realize their influence. "Human beings, who are almost unique in having the ability to learn from the experience of others, are also remarkable for their apparent disinclination to do so." (~Douglas Adams) All too often I have lived the second half of this quote. We all know versions of the cliché family that compliments Adams' wisdom: I needed these experiences in order to be where I now am, that experience made me who I am, good to get that experience under your belt, if it doesn't kill you it makes you stronger. Think about this family of clichés for a moment. Most of us have used them and there is a place for their concept. I used one when I rented one of my apartment units to a tenant that I probably knew I should not have. I'll share a bit of that story, despite the risk of you deciding that I have needed too many frying pans for you to read further!

The couple that responded to the advertised apartment seemed nice and close enough to normal, whatever that might mean. Steve was a contractor who worked regularly with some of the large home improvement companies, installing siding and gutters. His van was very well-organized and he had enough cash on hand to cover the deposit and first months' rent. This was before craigslist and easy online apartment listings, so finding potential tenants usually required – some readers may need to brace for this shocking reality – actually paying for an ad in a printed newspaper. This had several implications. First, the ad only lasted so long. Second, the fee was not inconsequential. Third, I was traveling quite a bit with consulting work, so I needed to get this apartment filled within a few days or it might have to wait another month or longer, sitting empty. I'm not sure where all the wiring originated, but I am certain now that my brain has hardwiring that fundamentally resists waste. Yes, let's jump on yet another overused cliché that blames the wiring in my brain. More on that later. All of these factors collaborated to give me a feeling that I should get the place rented asap (like just about everything else in my life at that point). As a handy contractor, my new tenant Steve could help with another challenge of being an absentee landlord. At the time, I lived several states away from the property; Steve could take care of the lawn, snow removal, and be the unofficial handyman for the other three units in the building. Now we've got a partially perfect picture. Steve's girlfriend, Linda, seemed to be a bit of a different story. She had children from a different relationship. Linda had other things going on, and did not seem to fit the ideal tenant mold from my real estate books and seminar. That would be fine, though, because she was not going to be on the lease. Steve would be on the lease alone. Linda's children would only stay on occasion. Now you are worried about me. So am I. It pains me to write these words. I spent years trying to pretend this scenario never happened or, better yet, that it was a necessary experience to help me learn a lesson. That's exactly where the cliché took me. For a few years, everything was pretty good with the whole arrangement. Steve was great with taking care of all the things that can easily make a rental property several states away tremendously fun and expensive: he fixed leaky faucets, reset the furnace when it shut off during the coldest week of the decade, kept the lawn in good shape, and always paid on time. Then, without much warning to me, Steve moved out. Okay, Steve was kicked out might be a more appropriate description. Yes, let's use that. However, I did not do the kicking. Linda took care of that. Since Steve was on the lease and Linda was not, one that is ignoring almost all forms of common sense might assume that Linda should also naturally move out. That is not exactly how the story proceeds for our brave and noble "I need these experiences to be where I am today" protagonist. Linda and company (some unverifiable number of children and animals included, who, by the way, were also not on the lease) thought they should camp in my building for as many months as were comfortable. Comfortable encompassed another word Linda seemed to like: free. When this "experience that I needed to be where I am today" came to its splendid conclusion, the cost of the lesson amounted to more than the cost of the real estate seminar, all the real estate books, and a good percentage of the rent that Steve had so faithfully paid over their time as tenants. Jonathan, you ask, why do you share this? We will now never go into business with you. Allow a brief aside. So many of our society's experts try to present themselves as having never failed, never made mistakes. My favorite mentors and leaders in history have been able to say they were off track, perhaps dramatically off track. Authenticity shouldn't be like the diet soda cycle described earlier!

Why do I share this? First, my therapist (who happens to also be hardwired into my brain and share this book's author's name) believes my laughter over the issue will help my journey. Okay, all kidding aside. I share it because we do not always need to make every mistake or experience every instance with such a high price tag in order to truly learn some of the most valuable lessons. We can, and probably should much more than we currently do, take lessons from legends. We can get those lessons much quicker than most of us do if we seek them and refute the cliché, "I need these experiences to be where I am today."

This highly interesting trap in life goes something like this: all of my experiences helped me get to where I am now. Yes. BUT...

one could have evaluated these experiences more rapidly, attained their lessons that much quicker and, as a result, been able to serve more people sooner. Don't take this pessimistically. Take it as a lesson going forward. What if going forward can be an unbelievably powerful question. *"What if?"* looking back can be debilitating, unless it's used to course correct today and tomorrow.

That was all part of the idea of creating Entrepreneur Adventure's immersion programs. We can and should learn the big lessons of life sooner and with a high degree of intentionality. The American culture does not fool around with helping first grade children learn to read. Reading has an intense focus. They will learn to read. Ella's first grade teacher reiterated that point on Parent Night and in Parent Teacher conferences. All the children will know these 100 words by the end of this year. Rigor. Intentionality. Entrepreneur Adventure would accelerate the process with a twist. The attendees would learn to be clear about their life's mission by the end of the week. They would get other lessons, as well, but this clarity of life's mission would happen.

Who am I? What do I stand for? As a result, what will I do with my life? These questions and their specific order come from years of my personal quest and are borrowed from some of the greatest minds and philosophers throughout history. From a practical approach, I have met too many people who followed these questions in the reverse order, starting with "What will I do with my life" and often letting that answer dictate or overpower the first two questions. The career or line of work doesn't seem to matter. I've met many, many entrepreneurs and aspiring entrepreneurs who start with their version of the third question (What will I do with my life?): "What business should I start?"

One translation: what might make some money or might work as a business.

How does our culture create this pattern of reversing the questions for so many people? My experience might just be in line with millions of others in this area. I grew up with several role models who daily demonstrated two starkly different models.

The first model: you love your work; it contributes tremendous value to society, and pays almost nothing. The second, and opposite, alternative was also effectively demonstrated: you hate your work; it just feeds a global economic engine, but affords you a decent lifestyle. "You gotta work." Pick one. The question may never have been posed directly.

Two conversations that never happened go something like this:

> *"Jonathan, you just go out there and use your unique talents and gifts to change the world. It will make your heart sing. Like Mama always says, you gonna be broke but you gonna be happy!"*

> *"Jonathan, what you want to do is find something you'll be miserable doing. Those are the jobs that pay well. You may not be great at it or enjoy it, but it'll put food on the table. That's the real world. Someday we all have to wake up and join it."*

Did these conversations happen for you? I'm not actually sure that they didn't occur many times and in many versions. What are you going to do when you grow up becomes a theme question that everyone asks. "Who are you?" and "What do you stand for?" are much less often heard.

This is an area where religions, scientific beliefs, philosophies all too often focus on their differences rather than step back to see where they overlap. In all honesty, my eyes have glossed over plenty of times in my life when someone would tell me that God has a plan for my life. I was in science mode. Today, I'm often tempted to share that same advice, despite knowing that the recipient may be exactly where I once was. Let's try to step back for a moment on this powerful question of the purpose of life. Much of the world would say that you and I were created

> "To be nobody but yourself in a world which is doing its best, night and day, to make you everybody else means to fight the hardest battle which any human being can fight; and never stop fighting."
> ~ E. E. Cummings

with a purpose, handmade by a Master Craftsman. More than half the world's population follows an Abrahamic religion, and therefore, share the scripture Jeremiah 29:11 "I know the plans I have for you, says the Lord, plans of good and not of evil, plans to give you a future and a hope." Others would say that we are nothing more than a product of an unbelievably complex evolutionary process, survival of the fittest. Many today would argue that the miracle of our existence comes from the combination of both processes. Rather than argue the points of each, let's take a very simple approach. If I were created, did my Creator have a purpose in mind? If I were a product of scientific evolution with no Intelligent Design, wouldn't survival of the fittest and that evolutionary process have gifted me to be very good at something important for survival? Either way, the question of what was I built for seems to be a very valid one. Hence, Who am I? Einstein made many brilliant comments. One of my favorites: "We are all born geniuses. But if you judge a fish on its ability to climb a tree, it will live its whole life believing that it is an idiot." Corporate America's version: "if your company's mission is climbing trees, do you hire squirrels or hire elephants and train, coach, mentor and put them all on corrective action and personal improvement plans?" Part of the first question, then, becomes in what areas were you born a genius? What were you built for? What makes your heart sing? What were you not built for? What does not make your heart sing? Both sides are important to work out. Recall the discussion early in the book about 2,000,000 18-year-old's heading off to college without having really worked this out. Is figuring out who you are and what you stand for given the same level of rigor as learning to read in elementary school? One might say that learning to read will facilitate the life purpose search. Perhaps. Is it worthy of a similar level of intentionality, or should it be left to a more subtle approach, hoping that the future leaders of the world figure it out?

The TPS Model: What did Ford, the Wrights, Edison and Gandhi all have in common?

After years of trying to decipher the riddle of what I should do with my life, I had arrived at the overlapping circle model shown below.

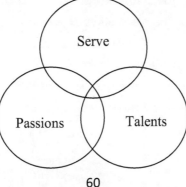

Summarized in a sentence, how can I use my talents and passions to serve? T P S. The model goes hand in hand with the three questions in the prior section. The model simply becomes a challenge of figuring out what fits in each of the circles and then working out the overlap. I don't believe this can be done

> "Where your talents and the needs of the world cross; there lies your vocation."
> ~ Aristotle

properly without living the principle of applied teachability from the previous chapter. Even though the model made sense from a logical perspective, I still struggled with something psychologists call cognitive dissonance, simply translated as trying to act in a manner that doesn't agree with what you believe to be true. A great example of this from my early experimentation with the model might clarify this dissonance.

I was consulting for one of the largest companies in the world, but was itching to build my own business. What kind of business should I start? Well, I had done roofing for 3 summers through college. The roofing business could pay fairly well, there would always be demand, and I had developed some skill at the work. Perfect. Oh, one more thing. I didn't really like roofing work – at all. Affordable Roofing is born in Canton, MI. My older brother and I (about a year before the car accident) printed fliers and drove around neighborhoods, putting a flier in each mailbox linked to a home that looked in need of a new roof. We were well on our way. The first call came in for an estimate. This is going to be too easy. My brother already had a ladder, tape measure, paper, and a calculator. All we would need now is a truck to get the ladder to the house. Despite our prospect living just a few blocks away, budding entrepreneurs that we were, our instincts told us that walking a few blocks with the ladder and telling the potential customer that we lived right around the corner might not help our credibility. Our finely honed business senses also warned us that pulling up to the house with the ladder strapped to the car roof might negatively impact our credibility as experienced roofers. Borrow a truck? Yes, borrow a truck! That was the obvious answer and that is precisely what we did. We then proceeded to measure that roof like it was nobody's business. We measured and re-measured, creating a perfectly scaled architect's view of the roof with every supply estimated, including number of nails. We then wrote up our estimate and delivered it, once again with the borrowed truck. Incorporate? What? Signage? Why? We never heard back from this customer and had to admit that we were fairly relieved. The idea of roofing houses after work and on weekends wasn't really something either of us had any interest in. Cognitive dissonance, once again, is trying to act differently than you believe or feel. My brother and I both believed that you make money and build a business doing things you didn't necessarily like. Was that why we picked roofing? If you don't really like doing it, it must pay well. That was one of my early attempts at the Talents and Passions to Serve model, obviously violating the Passions circle in the model. Could I be the only one with this dissonance? I don't know about that.

Manpower reported in 2010 that "find a new job" topped Americans New Year's resolution lists, with 84% listing it. Yahoo! Finance and Parade reported in September, 2012 that 60% in a survey of 26,000 people reported that they wanted to change careers. We probably don't need a survey to tell us this answer. Just look around. How many people do you know who are truly passionate about what they do? Similar statistics might verify that many of us operate outside of our greatest talents most of our lives. From where does this dissonance come? The two conversations that never happened from the previous section would be part of my answer. The second part, and the part that makes me, and perhaps you more than a bit uncomfortable as parents, big brothers or sisters, or older cousins: you and I want those who look up to us to live following this model. Follow your passion. Use your gifts. Serve. The mirror is an amazing invention. I have a younger brother and now two young daughters. I had to look in that mirror and ask, "If I were watching me, would I see a person that is using his talents and passions to serve?" Uncomfortable moments for me when I've asked that question.

Okay, so I want to follow the model but have often violated the model, along with much of the civilized world. Grow up, Jonathan, I have been told on many occasions when discussing this model. You might be thinking along similar lines. It's a great model, but the world just doesn't work that way. My daughters love library adventures, and on one such adventure, I had the chance to share my three overlapping circles model. We have so many great libraries around the country and at least a dozen within a half hours' drive of my home. Some weeks we'll make several library adventures together, traveling to the one with the giant fish tank, the puppets, or the rabbit doll house. Two year old Maya calls it the Rabbit "Wibelly". On one of these visits, while my girls were immersed in play, I got into a discussion with another parent about the usual introductory topics, how old the kids are, do they sleep at night, where do they go to school, what kind of work are you involved in... As part of the what do you do formality, I was giving this mother an overview of the Entrepreneur Adventure program and the overlapping circles model when another nearby mother overheard and joined our conversation. She said it sounded awesome, amazing, lovely, idealistic, like an amazing fairytale, and that I must have a spouse that does real work to support my hobby. Think about this for a moment. How would you respond to your prized model being under attack? It wasn't just under attack, it was now a cute little puppy that would someday grow up and realize that someone had to pay for dog food and vet visits. This is your chance. Do you really buy the model enough to try to defend it against that? Sure, the defense might be a silent internal debate that lasts for several days or weeks, but would you be ready for the debate? Is it a fairy tale? Can the world really work with this model or is it just for a very select few, the LeBron James', Jim Carrey's, and Picasso's of the world? Isn't that a question you really need to answer? I recently heard the statement, all models are false, some are useful. It made sense to me. We come across models all the time. The way a government should work, the way a school system should work, the TPS overlapping circles introduced here. None are perfect. Some are useful. We'll talk more in depth about beliefs in a later chapter, but I needed to work on my belief in / or disbelief in / this model. Knowing that you have to win the debate over the philosophies that you build your life around keeps you on your toes. I knew this debate was coming, whether in my head or in the real world, so I had done some homework. The homework and the debate weren't really about someone else questioning my seedling philosophy. They were about me questioning my seedling philosophy. I use seedling because new ideas, new visions, new dreams, new ways of approaching life are like tiny seedlings. Ella and I decided to grow apple trees one year. We had to put the seeds in the refrigerator to simulate winter, get them to believe they had made it through winter and spring was en route. Then we planted them, watered them, and watched them not grow. Yes, not grow. My Opa's green thumb skipped me altogether. However, if the seeds would have grown, they start as tiny seedlings, extremely delicate and able to be plucked out of the soil by anyone who happens by. That's true for any new approach you see and try to adopt. Knowing this and preparing for this, I had started to research some of the legends throughout history to see how the model might stack up. With only a small degree of facetiousness, I tell you I was actually shocked by what I found. The Wright Brothers: they LOVED flying! Henry Ford: he was totally into cars! Gandhi was passionate about a free and independent India. Martin Luther King, Jr. cared deeply about civil rights for all humanity. Thomas Edison practically lived in his Menlo Park laboratory, loving every moment. Michael Jordan has an obsession with playing basketball: he even had a "love of the game" clause built into his contract, allowing him freedom to play in pick-up games whenever he chose. Houdini was totally into magic. In fact, Pat Williams (COO of the Orlando Magic, former GM of the Philadelphia Phillies and Seventy-sixers) writes that the secret to success is to "figure out what you love to do as young as you can and then organize your life around figuring out how to make a living at it." Williams doesn't just provide a great quote, he lives it. He always loved sports, but his talent only took him to baseball's minor leagues. Passion: sports. Talent: Marketing & Leading People. Serve: He got involved managing a minor league baseball team and worked his way up quickly. Another line from Pat Williams: "You can only fake passion for about two weeks."

Did the legends figure out ways to serve? You can answer that one. Henry Ford put America on wheels. He initiated the $5/day pay, enabling every worker in his factories to afford a Ford. Andrew Carnegie (once the wealthiest person in the world) had these words inscribed on his tombstone, "Here lies a man who knew how to enlist the service of better men than himself." When asked his role in the steel empire, Carnegie's responded that his role was to ensure a spirit of harmony. Another line that Carnegie and Warren Buffet both liked to use pertains to our model. "Put all your eggs in one basket and then watch the basket." Buffett (the most successful investor in history) says he missed the play on cellular phone stocks because it's not within his core competency – his Talent. I'll spare you the rest of the homework, but will share the other side of the debate that played in my mind. Could the model work for the whole world? It's the "is someone built for each and every job?" question. It could be rephrased as "are there people whose TPS circles overlap on every societal role?" Tough question. I will not pretend to have a complete answer to that just yet. My take, however, is simply this: not enough people will buy in to the model for us to get to that point. The other part of my philosophy around this question says that "Who are you BECOMING?" supersedes the TPS circles. In other words, any role can help you to become, even if you are not yet operating within your overlap. To me, it is quite inspiring to think about the impact of a few more people deciding to use their talents and passions to serve. Another way to look at the question: what great services to the world have not been done because people did not live within this model?

Wilber's two great objects change the world

William Wilberforce (known by close friends as Wilber) radically changed the modern world. He was one of the most influential people of the last 300 years, yet many do not know his name or story today. Abe Lincoln and Frederick Douglas agreed that every school child in America should learn about his contribution. You may be familiar with the movie, Amazing Grace, which shares a part of Wilber's story. Wilber had met Benjamin Franklin in Paris several years before writing out his two great objects. Perhaps Franklin explained the 13 week plan for virtuous living to Wilberforce? I have been unable to verify. Wilber's family was quite wealthy, and the deaths of his grandfather and uncle when William was in his late teens left Wilberforce independently wealthy. While avoiding study at Saint James College in Cambridge, Wilber began a lifelong friendship with classmate and future prime minister, William Pitt. Wilberforce and Pitt began career in parliament while still in college, and Wilberforce quickly became renowned for his gift of oratory. Throughout his first quarter century of life, Wilberforce struggled between a life guided by deep spiritual convictions and a hedonistic lifestyle. It was during this struggle that Wilberforce sought the mentorship of John Newton, former slave ship captain turned clergyman and author of the moving song *Amazing Grace* about his own spiritual struggles at sea in his slave ship after a terrible storm. A young Wilberforce was haunted by the question: if he lived out his developing spiritual convictions, must that end his political career? Both Newton and Pitt advised Wilbur to maintain his political career.

At the age of 28, in 1787, Wilberforce penned these words in his journal: "God Almighty has set before me two great objects: the suppression of the slave trade and a reformation of morals." He felt that God was leading him to end slave trade and bring the British Empire back to morals, or a character focus. At the time he wrote this, Wilberforce was a rising star in British parliament, considered by many to be in line for the job of Prime Minister. He was a gifted orator and had a natural charisma, energy, and charm. When this new vision for his life started to take hold of him, he wrestled with the idea of leaving his position in parliament, actually leaving politics all together, to dedicate his life to this social cause. How can I SERVE? He knew the causes he would serve, but how? To get just a sense of Britain's moral state at this time, one in four unmarried women in London were prostitutes.

> "You may choose to look the other way but you can never say again that you did not know."
> ~ William Wilberforce

Friends convinced him to keep his post and use his oratory gift to bring this vision to reality. The answer to How can I serve was the TPS model. He used his natural gift and passions for oratory and helping his fellow man to begin a long and costly campaign to fulfill those two great objects.

After fighting tirelessly to affect these two causes, and just three days before his death on July 29, 1833, Wilberforce heard news that the British Empire would officially pass the Bill for the Abolition of Slavery. William Wilberforce had truly given his life for this cause. He had found his authentic swing, his way to use his Talents and Passions to Serve.

Applied Teach-ability and the three circles

Let's dig into combining the first two principles, Applied Teach-ability and Clarity of Vision. Here is the process of finding my own unique overlap of the three circles in two recent ventures.

Example #1: Entrepreneur Adventure

Since I have started well over a dozen businesses (some as short-lived as a few weeks, like Affordable Roofing, but all packed full of lessons), I have long wished there were a program that let people really see what it's like to start their own business. The lessons of having something for which you are completely responsible are

> "Feedback is the breakfast of champions."
> ~ Ken Blanchard

numerous and significant. Somewhere around mid-May of 2010, I was thinking about the idea again and my own words kept coming back to me. "Why not get started today? You learn almost nothing about a business until you have some skin in the game. Do it now – this summer – and you'll learn more in the next few months than you could learn from years of merely thinking about it. Get in the game. Get feedback." How often have I had great advice for someone else while I was busy not following the same advice in my own life! This would not be one of those times. I got committed. Some form of Business Camp would be conducted that very summer. Where? When? How? Who? No idea, but the commitment was 100%. It would happen. I started talking about the camp to everyone I knew. One friend offered to help. Perfect. Now it's June. When will we schedule the camp? Summer is so short and it was already about to start. High schools were finishing up already. We needed time to plan, figure out a location, let people know we're running a camp – to name just a few of the endless items to get done. July was too soon. That leaves August. Did I forget to mention that my wife, Dominika, was pregnant with our second child, Maya, and was due on August 16th? Welcome to the wives out there, whose husband just handed them the book to prove that there are other husbands that make some crazy choices! Now, everyone knows that the second child is always born early. That meant early

August was out. Naturally the last week of August, rolling into September was too late because kids are getting ready for back to school. That left Monday through Friday, the week of August 23rd through 27th. That should work. We had our dates. We'll get back to the rest of the story in a moment, but allow me to finish the Maya story for the husband-wife teams reading together. Maya's due date, Monday August 16th, arrived without any sign of Maya joining the outside world. To this day, I still think Dominika handled it like a true champ. No anxiety. Tuesday, Wednesday, Thursday, Friday, Saturday – no Maya just yet. Sunday morning – no Maya. August 23rd, Entrepreneur Adventure Summer Camp 2010 Day 1, is less than 24 hours away. We were at a friend's house for a birthday party and Dominika wanted to leave a little early. Back home, she went to sleep early while I looked through some last minute adjustments to Monday's curriculum and printed some of the program materials. Roughly 12:23am on Monday, August 23rd, Dominika woke up and thought a trip to the hospital might be a good idea. Okay, we can do that. A few hours later, at approximately 7:00am, the doctor lets us know that everything is going great. 7:45am... Maya Fanning makes her entrance. 9:00am... EA Camp Day 1 begins, location just 7 minutes away from the hospital. Yes, that's about how it happened. Note, if Maya ever gets her hands on a copy of this book, please remove this page, or pour chocolate syrup over this section. Thanks! By this point in the book, you know that I am seriously considering revising this section, but you probably also know me well enough to realize that I am not trying to convince you that I am perfect, or that I haven't made plenty of mistakes. My little growing family had also just moved into a new house, and renovated extensively between May and August... But that's a story that we don't need to expand upon here. You can probably imagine the lack of simplicity!

Back to June and camp planning. Who would attend was our next question. That would dictate the curriculum development, marketing, price, and location. Teens? High School Students? College Students? Well-off financially? Low income? Anyone and everyone who had a genuine interest in starting a business? We narrowed it down to teens and got to work. As you can imagine, a lot more decisions had to be made and it took a tremendous amount of work to pull this together in about two months, while also working on our real businesses. What a crazy idea. But it really happened. The experience that those inaugural teens had absolutely changed the way they look at the world. One of them called me a few months ago for some guidance and talked to me for about an hour about how many lessons from that experience still guide him today.

Let's take Clarity and TPS around the camp experience through Applied Teach-ability.

Passion: check. Talent: hmmm – not perfect. Serve: check, but something was a little off. Dissect the experience. Examine life. That first camp wasn't exactly in the overlap of the circles for me. What was off? Working with that group in the manner that we did for 5 full days straight was not really within my talent/serve overlap. What was off, though? Was it just that I didn't have the skills honed yet? Perhaps. Or was it the age? Maybe. It could have even had something to do with sleep deprivation from my new little angel, Maya. I couldn't be sure, but had certainly learned tremendous lessons about which exercises left the greatest impact, which were not for that particular group, and which needed some degree of tweaking. Three of the many definite keepers: having the teens compete in a real business project to finance their own lunch, business plan presentation via live streaming video that their families and friends could watch, and a very moving ceremony of leaving a habit behind and replacing it with a better habit. It would take several iterations of the Entrepreneur Adventure experience, experimenting with many aspects, including different demographics of high school students, college students, MBA students, and high school drop-outs to enhance the clarity of the TPS overlapping circles. Part of my Talent and Passion overlap included the vision behind the programs and taking tremendous experiential learning concepts and translating them into entrepreneurial lessons. Creating the experiential learning exercises from scratch, however, was not within my Talent circle.

Example #2: EQ Workshops for Parents and Teachers

I had been speaking and holding training workshops on several topics, including creativity, leadership development, and the very popular topic of emotional intelligence (EI or Emotional Quotient - EQ). Someone wise once said the best way to learn a topic is to teach it. The more I taught about EQ, the more I would see the impact of this topic on my life as an entrepreneur, as a friend, as a family member, as a husband, as a parent, as a person. Emotional Intelligence can be simply defined as awareness and management of emotions in self and others. This simple definition presents an amazing challenge to modern life. If you'll reflect throughout the day on the recipes involved in your changing emotional states and your effectiveness or ineffectiveness at impacting your emotional state in varied life situations, you may feel the same intrigue about this topic that I do. After studying the topic in depth, leading dozens of workshops, and trying to apply what I was learning to my own life, including my parenting, I had a growing concern over the modern world's declining EQ. Everyone needs this, especially parents and others who work with young children. Like so many challenges, affecting this one early on in the process and providing tools and mindsets to children would equip them for a lifetime. How could I help my children build their own EQ, even at their young ages? Another quest was beginning. What if they could be building their EQ starting today, instead of waiting until they were in their 30's or 40's? I dove in and found tools, strategies, exercises, language, and hope. While still very much in quest mode, seeking answers while trying to apply those I had already found, the seed of an idea to teach this to preschool teachers, daycare providers, and other parents began rapidly growing roots in my mind. Through a children's fitness and birthday party business that I had built (and will discuss further in the next section), I had witnessed hundreds of parents and childcare providers struggling with affecting their emotions and those of their children all too often. One frequent occurrence: a parent would instantly instill cowardice in a child through one emotionally intense look. I am not referring to "the look" of put that down or did you just hit your baby sister. This look would say "you are deathly afraid of climbing that rock wall!" Without getting into a discourse on EQ, emotions can be extremely contagious, especially during eye contact between parent or caregiver and child. What emotions do you pour into the children (and adults) around you? That same glance can instill courage, confidence, warmth, love, belief. After observing, experiencing, and now beginning to understand the science behind this powerful concept, I had to teach others who had children or worked with children. A stake was being hammered into the ground. A workshop would happen – with whom, how, what, when, where – these had all become semantics.

In order to best understand the next steps in this process, I want to borrow a story from Jim Collins, author of *Good to Great* and many other outstanding books that deal with business, leadership, and life. Imagine that you and I are sailing on an old wooden ship. Most of my audiences decide that we should be pirates, so we'll go with that. We are pirates sailing the Caribbean in the 1700's. Suddenly, you spy a ship in the distance and it has turned towards our ship. Through the spyglass, you see that it is one of the fastest ships in the feared British Navy. It will catch us and will be well-armed. Our band of pirates is in trouble. "Ready the cannons!" you bark to the crew. One of the crew quietly and nervously approaches you, stammering something about gunpowder. "Speak up!" you shout. Apparently our pirate ship has enough gunpowder left to fire ONE substantial cannonball, but not quite enough to fire two. At this point, most pirates would load up that one cannon and aim for quite some time. Fire would be ordered but once, and this command would be issued either too early or too late. That single cannonball might be launched well before the British ship had begun firing on us. On the other hand, our cannonball might be launched after 30 were launched from the British ship. Either way, it would likely miss. That's how the story for most pirates in our situation would end, but thanks to your wisdom - and we are only here to write about this because of your wisdom – you decide to mount a musket next to that cannon. Then you take very small portion of the gunpowder and fire a bullet from the musket, taking careful note of its trajectory. High and to the left. Adjust. Fire another bullet. Adjust. Fire another bullet. Adjust. Fire another bullet. After a dozen or so adjustments, you load the remaining powder into the cannon, fire, and sink the British vessel. Well done. My children's children thank you. Jim Collins calls this "Fire bullets, then cannonballs."

My first, second, third, fourth … workshops on "Emotional Intelligence for Parents and Teachers" were born precisely this way. With the seedling of this idea growing, I visited a daycare customer for my children's fitness business. After our program, I could have departed, but thought to myself, no, I'll go speak with the director. In that conversation, I subtly mentioned being busy and leading workshops for helping childcare workers with Emotional Intelligence. Her response: "Really? That would be great for one of my staff meetings." She asked about my availability about two weeks from then. We scheduled a 90 minute program and I went home thinking what exactly will I cover? The workshop went extremely well and led to a referral to work with a group of childcare providers. Before that initial conversation, I did not have a proposal template, a finalized curriculum, download-able EQ Exercises for Childcare Providers online, a website that mentioned EQ programs for childcare, a brochure, or even a business card related to this topic. Bullets then cannonballs. Feedback. Applied Teach-ability leading to clarity of vision. Who did I want to work with? How? Where? That wasn't completely clear for this workshop yet, but getting in the game and anticipating feedback made the process happen in a few weeks. Please don't interpret this as doing something half way or dabbling. In a sense, it may be likened to dabbling with a purpose that is becoming ever clearer. Beginning purpose (sink British vessel): help children build their EQ.

- Bullet 1: workshop with daycare teachers.
- Bullet 2: add a dozen exercises that can be done in a preschool or elementary school.

- Bullet 3: mix theory & high level understanding with many applications for teachers and children.
- Bullet 4: very brief on theory/concepts and guide teachers to create application, spoon feeding examples when necessary.
- Bullet 5: add online video and download to reinforce and go deeper.
- Bullet 6: workshop for PTA at large public school.
- Bullet 7: online video series for parents and childcare providers.
- Cannonball time?

Too many times in my life I had followed, like so many in our culture, the opposite approach. Cannonball 1st and nothing left for bullets. I bought two, yes TWO, franchises almost simultaneously. Neither was totally in line with my overlapping circles. I still doubted the overlapping circles model at the time and will discuss this more deeply in the next section. Marketing materials, target audience, products and services were all set, not allowing much room for applied teach-ability. Selection of a college major often follows the same philosophy. What will I do with my life is a pretty big question to answer with one cannonball. I am very thankful today for my mother's wisdom and guidance of encouraging an informal internship with a doctor my freshman year. That was a bullet. I believe one major overhaul in our educational system has to find a way to help young people, well before the age of 18, to incorporate this applied teach-ability towards finding overlaps in these three circles. The "dabbling" with feedback would probably need to be around a framework. What are my unique gifts? In what areas could I be one of the best in the world? I see plenty of parents helping their children dabble, but without a British vessel to hone their child's aim. This could easily be the topic of another book and we are currently considering the creation of a version of Entrepreneur Adventure immersion programs that would solely emphasize creating clarity of vision.

One challenge you can take from this section: find ways to easily and inexpensively taste-test the areas of life that may be the overlap of your three circles, Talent, Passion, Service. Help those around you to do the same. If you've always dreamed of owning a café, go work in one part time and become the best employee that place has ever had. Get as close as you can to playing the role of the owner. Evaluate that part time experience. Want to write a book? Write a few hundred words every day for a week and evaluate the experience. Dream of speaking to large audiences? Give four talks over the next month as a volunteer on topics that matter to you. Experiment with slight variations on audience, topic, timeframe, etc. Then try to charge for one. Make a little feedback sheet for the participants and have a trusted friend attend to provide additional feedback. List all the things you do well. A friend or family member might be very helpful, as we tend to think things we do well are easy for everyone else and, as a result, often downplay our own giftedness. Do the same with all the things that stir up passion in you. What makes you dream? What makes you cry? What keeps you up at night or gets you to jump out of bed in the morning? Two of my examples: learning about topics that could help others and giving speeches that challenge and inspire the audience to change the way they look at the world. Hence the title of many of my talks and programs: "Who are you BECOMING? Who are you helping those around you to BECOME?"

Simmer in Silence

I need to address something I have come to believe is a myth, an idea that I, and countless others, let hinder our creation of a clear vision. The myth is simple: the heroes, leaders, and legends magically know what they are supposed to do. They are either born with this clear vision or it strikes them one day. The Wright Brothers just knew they would do something with flying. Walt Disney knew he would build a movie and entertainment empire. Winston Churchill knew he would lead the world away from tyranny. Abe Lincoln knew he would lead the nation. I had to do some investigation of this "knowing." What exactly did they know and when did they know it?

September, 1919.

Walter Elias Disney is not quite 18 years old and has just returned from World War One. His father, Elias is excited because he has just invested $25,000 in the O'Zell Jelly Company. After dinner, Elias informs his son that he has arranged a good job for young Walt in the jelly factory, earning a cool $25 per week. Walt's simple response: "Dad, I don't want to work in the jelly factory. I want to draw cartoons." Elias answered in a paraphrase of what so many fathers have told their young dreamers, "You need to get a real job." Walt: "I will. I'll draw cartoons for the newspaper." Was Walt already dreaming? Absolutely. Did he know that he would build a theme park empire, audio animatronics, the first full length feature cartoon movie? I haven't found any evidence to support this level of clarity in the teenage Walt Disney. He was absolutely dreaming, and dreaming big. But his dreams evolved over time. He watered them, gave them sunlight, exposed them to so many others' dreams, chased a few dreams down, and created increasing

78

clarity over time. You can call it simmering, or borrow from leadership expert John Maxwell and call it *Crockpotting*. To me, creating clarity of vision is like making chili. My wife makes several versions of amazing chili. When she gets started, I hover around the kitchen, salivating for the

> **"Efforts and courage are not enough without purpose and direction."**
> **~ John F. Kennedy**

first taste. If I tried a spoon full of that great mix when the cooking has just begun, the taste would absolutely not work. Spices haven't soaked in. Flavors haven't enhanced each other yet. Give that chili a few hours on the stove and now we're getting somewhere. Delicious. A few more hours and the flavor is now somehow multiplied. If you want the most amazing flavor though, you let the chili cool, sit overnight, and reheat it a day or two later. Simmer. Crockpot. Make chili.

Creating your vision and the vision for an organization is very similar. Too many companies and individuals fall into the same trap that I had fallen into, believing that a clear vision is just created one day. The company schedules an off-site meeting and crafts a vision, mission statement, and organizing values. Great. Just like that first spoon full of chili. For a large portion of my life, I was expecting that I should one day get this tremendous clarity, so I waited for it. Over time, I came to realize that the light at the end of the tunnel is often only there to help you see the next step. It may not always illuminate the end of the tunnel for you. I remember hiking a railroad trail in Pennsylvania as a teenager. The trail led to so many adventures, but the most exhilarating for my older brother and I had to be the long dark tunnel to nowhere. The abandoned train tracks headed into the mountain and a mysterious darkness. We walked a few strides into the tunnel and then came back out. A second venture led us further into the darkness, and this time we could see a small pinhole of light far off in the distance. It was barely visible at first, but quickly became the only thing we could see beyond shadows a few yards away from us. Ultimately, that light at the end of our tunnel adventure only illuminated our next few steps and the direction to fresh air. When we reached the other side of the tunnel, the path disappeared. The railway exited the side of the mountain where it had once traversed a high wooden bridge, which was now just a skeleton of that bridge. We didn't take many steps on the old faded wooden frame, but we had made it. I think that tunnel adventure is very similar to the creation of a person's vision as well as an organization's vision. It likely won't be crystal clear at the start. Sometimes a simple framework or idea is enough. Using my talents and passions to serve became my framework, my light at the end of the tunnel that allowed just enough light to see my next few steps. Start a business that helps people to BECOME was one of those steps. Exactly who that business would serve and how were still a few steps beyond my view at that point. Keep the framework. Keep looking towards the end of the tunnel. It will become increasingly clear.

Many of the companies that I work with have struggled in a similar way. We have this vision, but it's not really that clear or compelling. Our team all but ignores it now. Why not try this: start with a simple word or phrase that can act as the framework, the light at the end of the tunnel, and head towards that. Pick something that excites, engages, inspires. Several of my clients have agreed on the pursuit of becoming world class. Simple. Highly Effective. Does that sound a bit familiar? Have I mentioned this before? My wife and I incorporate this into our family. We want to be a world class family. A great family. An amazing family. Have an amazing marriage. Be world class parents. Notice that it didn't start out perfectly clear, but does it satisfy the framework? Does it excite, engage, inspire? Does it provide a light towards which we head? Absolutely. Then we cook that idea for a while, living with it, talking about it. We may walk away from it, letting it cool overnight so that we can reheat it and add a few more spices. "Taste the chili, let me know what it's missing," is one of the best requests my wife can give me! It was within this framework and looking for a light at the end of the tunnel that I started using the "Who am I BECOMING? Who am I helping those around me to BECOME?" questions. Take a few minutes several times over the course of the next few days and jot down some words, phrases, questions, images, role models that might become the light at the end of the tunnel for this phase of your life, family, business, or cause.

In one of my businesses, we started with "amazing experience" which evolved into "Disney-like experience" and was a very effective light at the end of the tunnel.

Another wrong ladder?
Ignore the frying pan again?

Hindsight is sometimes even better than 20/20. Just before Thanksgiving in 2006, I found myself the proud father of a big green bus, with two more on the way. Only it was not exactly mine and probably shouldn't have been. Looking back on this decision that led to multiple prolonged and repeated frying pan moments, I battle between trying to convince myself that I needed the lesson and knowing that I probably should have already learned this one. I was in that phase of starting to come to terms with this TPS overlapping circles model, but hadn't validated it as quickly as I could have. Okay, that's probably just my story. More likely history is that I knew that TPS was a good model but violated it regardless. You want the truth, Jonathan? You can't handle the truth! Thanks to Jack Nicholson in "A Few Good Men" for that outstanding line. I had stumbled upon a children's fitness franchise and the founders hired me to do a very brief project, helping them to grow their business. In getting to know the business, I saw that it seemed like a simple business and the mathematician in me ran all kinds of numbers. This could work. I could build this business as a purely passive income stream. Shortly before Christmas that year, I told the story to most of my friends, getting several of them excited. Before I proverbially asked Jack to tell me the truth, I had convinced two partners to invest with me and build the largest franchise within this organization. If any friend of mine had repeated back to me this overlapping circles philosophy that I had already been developing for quite some time, my only logical response would have been something like, "the truth? I can't handle the truth!" If more of my friends used the "Who am I helping those around me to BECOME?" question, this conversation would have happened and I might never have owned one, two, or three big green buses.

What exactly was this business all about? Our buses were bright green and had cartoon children on the outside. The seats had all been removed and the inside was set up like a miniature children's gymnastics center. Everything was padded, and we had a rock climbing wall, trampoline, gymnastics bar, rings, rope swing, rope ladder, trapeze, and other types of hanging apparatuses that could be hooked or unhooked from the ceiling within seconds. We brought structured fitness programs to preschools and daycares during the week and amazing birthday parties to children's homes on the weekends. We worked with young children, primarily between two and seven years old. Our Beatles moments occurred frequently, as one of our buses (while driving) will be tracked down by frantically waving parents. We would smile, open the window, and ask if we can help. Most simply ask, "What exactly do you do?"

Not long into the process, my partners and I found out what I think we knew but effectively pretended we did not know. You need to be in to what you are in to. We needed to really get to know what makes this green bus business go. The pedal on the right and one or two good employees to run the whole show wasn't quite cutting it. Why, oh why, is the easiest person to deceive so often the one in the mirror?

> "You can fake passion for about two weeks."
> ~ Pat Williams

A friend of mine once told me that being pretty good at a lot of things could be a curse, rather than a blessing. I no longer buy that, as I have come to believe that we're built on purpose for a purpose.

Let's run this green bus business through my TPS model.

Talent: working with young children, hiring and training staff that do so, marketing to daycares and parents. Check, sort of. I am okay at most of these. Pretty good with young children. Okay at marketing to that demographic now, but not so okay before the bus. Hiring and training childcare staff: not so good at all. I do love people and truly enjoy working with them. However, I do not like a front line direct supervisory role. The role requires too much hand-holding, too much repetition of expectations, too much checking in. Therefore, talent does not get a check. Could I be the best in the world at this? No.

Passion: I enjoy the challenge of making something work. I enjoy working with young children for certain amounts of time. I like the idea of children's fitness. Does it keep me up at night? Well, yes, but not out of joy! Does it make me cry, give me energy? Not really. Passion doesn't get a check either.

Serve: Do I want to serve this audience? Yes. In this way? Not exactly. My EQ workshops for parents and childcare providers are much more in line with the ways I was built to serve.

Do you think it might be worth running some of the activities you are currently involved in through this model? I like to ask the KWINKI question. Knowing What I Now Know I would ... get involved in this industry, business, non-profit or not? Can you handle the truth?

My week in the hospital after hanging off that bridge 106 feet above the ground had led to a decision to not waste life. To not live a life that was not mine. As I built this green bus business, I would occasionally find myself thinking back on that fateful night and ask if I was making the best use of this second chance. I didn't like the answer and too often just decided to stop asking the question rather than climb down from this ladder of a rapidly growing business that was not the right business for me. The next chapter will deal with how and why I was stuck.

Chapter 4

Becoming Courageous

Think about a moment in your life when you pursued something that mattered and required courage. Was it a moment of courage? Or sustained courage?

A few moments of courage so often have defined the next few months, years, or even decades of my life. A few moments. What if I chickened out in those moments? Reflecting on things that took courage, it has been a mix of taking action, asking others to take action (help, invest, commit, step up, challenge philosophy...), and saying no. I can't really say which have been harder or more frequent, but currently, saying no seems to be the most important and courage-dependent. Maybe you would like to practice saying it with me: "no ... No ... NO!" Some no's are bigger than others, aren't they?

Right at the beginning of high school junior year, the new kid moved to our school. I heard legendary tales about Abdul before I met him. Basketball. That was his game and he was the complete package. Shoot, pass, drive, play defense, and court smarts. He would dominate. Did you see that move Abdul made in intramurals? Rumors swirled. Would Abdul be our high school basketball team that year? I have to admit, I had some anxiety. Part of me said that all the talk was just hype. Part of me was worried about my role on the basketball team with this new force. Only a small part of me was excited about the potential of playing with a teammate of that caliber. I was supposed to be the team, not play second fiddle to some new transfer. Then, I met Abdul. It happened on the court at an early fall intramural basketball game. We were just shooting around, loosening up, and without warning, Abdul was shooting next to me. After I shot the ball, my eyes stopped short as Abdul grabbed the rebound and passed the ball back to me. We exchanged the standard cool and casual head nod, a basketball

> "Men don't follow titles, they follow courage."
> ~William Wallace
> (*Braveheart*)

acknowledgment that we each knew who the other was. After shooting around for a while, we briefly introduced ourselves before the first game of the afternoon began. I would get a few opportunities to guard the new guy that day and he lived up to the legends. This kid could play. What a ridiculous handle. He could score, but looked for his teammates first, almost every time. He scored when necessary. What would this mean for my season? "Abdul, I know the best places for pick-up games around here. Want to go together on Wednesday?" I wasn't sure that I really wanted to invite Abdul to play together. I wasn't sure that I wanted the extra competition. I wasn't yet seeing this new star player as an entirely positive thing. But that one brief moment of courage would set the stage for that whole year.

Abdul's family had relocated from Los Angeles and he lived and breathed basketball. Over the next few months, we played together constantly. We would hunt down the best outside pick-up games to be found. If the weather wasn't good, we'd be in the YMCA, working on moves, playing one-on-one, competing in shoot-outs, lifting weights, and even practicing our footwork in the pool. Footwork in the pool was new to me. The water resistance builds up your foot speed and coordination. Perhaps the hardest part of this dedication to taking our games to the next level was saying no. We said no to goofing off after school. We said no to going to movies on Friday nights. We said no to eating a lot of junk food. We said no to being tired. We said no to letting a few missed shots discourage us from these endless practice sessions. We said no to giving up after driving from one park to another to another, in search for the best pick-up competition. We said no to letting a car accident (a full-sized pick-up truck smashed into and totaled my car) en route to the CYC for pickup games slow us down. We said no over and over and over to many good things. How? We wanted basketball to be a great thing.

That courage to take a forward step or say no to a distraction is fed by your bigger reason. What is your bigger reason? What can you do to practice courageously saying no to distractions today?

When a brave person stands...

The aspiring EIT (Entrepreneur-In-Training) was just thirteen years old. Zack's team stared, with astonished faces as he stuttered and stammered on the phone. As he hung up, no one said a word to him. Zack was home-schooled and his older brother was also attending the camp. The two boys and their mother almost literally camped at the camp. They lived a few hours' drive from our location and stayed with my co-facilitator in his spare bedroom for the week. After Zack's first phone call, I wasn't sure if I should interrupt the moment for a teaching point or wait it out. While debating this in my mind, Zack started to dial again. He asked for the owner a bit more calmly this time. The owner wasn't available and Zack asked when might be a good time to call back. No time for a teaching point or even a mental debate this time around. Zack was back on the phone, calling a third café. This call went even more smoothly. Was our youngest Entrepreneur Adventure camper setting the bar for the rest of his group? After a few more calls, this thirteen-year-old was all smiles and high-fiving his whole group. Their initial shock had turned into awe-inspired enthusiasm and belief that a small group of teens could take on the world, perhaps even change the course of humanity. After all, hasn't it always been small groups of people with great courage that have changed the course of human events? These twenty minutes of phone calls were all part of an orchestrated EA camp module we had created called "Be Courageous!" During the module leading up to this, the campers had taken their ideas for their business model into a small list of actionable items that met two criteria:

Significant Progress:
Accomplishing these activities would move the business forward significantly.
Significant Courage:
The activities would require a good deal of courage from the Entrepreneur-In-Training.

Zack's business, created using the overlapping three circles (T P S), was a jazz band that would perform live and sell recorded audio. His #1 activity that met the above criteria: contact café's in his hometown that hire jazz bands for live performances. Once the EIT's finished creating these lists, their teams and EA facilitators challenge the list, qualifying the final

> "Tell me and I forget. Show me and I remember. Let me do and I understand."
> ~ Confucius

activities as significant in each of the two criteria. Some EIT's might replace an activity with one that would create greater progress. Then, we took a break before moving to this module. EIT's formed teams and had 1 hour to accomplish items that fit with their respective significant progress and significant courage lists. Zack was the first to take action in his group. Each day of our camp is dedicated to one skill and one character trait. The character trait for this day: courage. Zack's courage unleashed something amazing, inspiring, and predictable. When a brave soul stands, it stiffens the spines of those around. One of Zack's teammates, James, who just happened to be the oldest in the group and the most sophisticated, decided he could also take a bold action. He reached out to some contacts for investment capital for his startup software business. Although this response didn't come until that evening and wasn't reported to the group until the next morning, James received a pledge for $1,000 in startup seed money from a person he contacted in our "Be Courageous!" hour.

After witnessing this series of events, I began to think how different most of our lives would be today if we had one extra hour of "Be Courageous!" at some point in the last decade. Recall the formula C x S = QQL (Character x Skill = Quantity and Quality of Leadership) from earlier in the book. How much leadership value would your heroes have provided to the world without courage? My Opa came to this country at the age of 16. His father didn't like what was going on in Germany at the time and had the courage to get his family out, one person at a time, so as not to raise a flag that might extinguish the family's chances of escaping tyranny. Both my grandfather and his father needed courage to make this moment happen. A courageous decision supported by sustained courageous action. That type of courage can be found in the history of every family. How different would the world be if we each built this emphasis on courage into our daily life? There are so many ways to build this trait. I can schedule it into my calendar before the week starts. On Friday, before noon, I will contact ten potential clients that meet the criteria of significant progress and significantly scary. Each night, I could map out 3 courageous acts to take the next day. Each hour I could ask myself, what would be the right thing to do that would also require courage? A basketball coach could challenge the team to have a courageous phase in practice each day. Guard someone you normally would not, or dare to take three tough shots that you normally hesitate to take in the next drill or quarter.

Corporate meeting moderators could challenge the participants' courage on several fronts:

dare to be brutally honest
dare to show appreciation
dare to set bigger goals
dare to admit you may be wrong
dare to put team's goals above your own
dare to delegate twice as much as you currently do
dare to challenge ideas that may need a second look

For me, I find that some of my most courageous moments hit me at 11 pm, or while I am driving to visit friends on the weekend, or at 3 am when the great idea gets me out of bed. I am ready to make it happen, take on the world, contact one of the world's largest companies and ask them to sponsor a "Let's Change the World Together" or "Who are you BECOMING?" speech, seminar, program, or tour. In those moments, I am so ready to make it happen. On a scale of one to ten, my courage is at a fourteen. I'm like the athlete that always goes out there and gives 110%. Off the charts. Let me at them! Somehow, over the next few days that unbelievable idea would make it to a list, but not necessarily be acted upon. What can I do about this? Take that moment of courageous inspiration and put it in the calendar with a completion time – while still in the moment of inspiration! Perhaps schedule something that inspires you before that task. I'll put things in my calendar like watch video from *Les Miserables* of "Do you hear the people sing."

BECOMING more courageous is a perfect match for the authentic swing concept introduced under "Applied Teach-ability." Do you find yourself a "be courageous" accountability partner that you text, call, or email each day? Do you make a "be courageous" journal? Do you plan your day's courageous acts the night or weekend before and set up miniature rewards for fulfilling the daily quota? One single week of becoming more courageous will have a life-changing effect. When will you start this?

Defining moments define your life

My first position after graduating from college was in a highly touted world-class leadership development program in a Fortune 500 company whose graduates have gone on to CEO roles in dozens of companies. Part of the program included four rotational job assignments, each lasting about 6 months. The program leads were supposed to help participants find their next role, but I thought it might be worth taking matters into my own hands. Where would my next assignment take me? After discussing options with the local program coordinator and hearing very limited open options, I had one of those courageously inspired ideas. I wouldn't look for an open job rotation. I would decide where I wanted to live and what work I wanted to do. I would then simply contact the person in charge at that location and let them know that I would be available shortly. Who might that person be? I found out quickly that the right person would be the Vice President of that division. There were several locations that caught my interest. Long Island, NY and Washington D.C. were the top two choices. So I simply began calling the respective VP's of operations in these areas. I'm not sure if I didn't know that this was not the way you were "supposed" to do it or that I realized that the "right way" to find my next rotation wouldn't get me the rotation that I wanted. Either way, it worked quite well. Did those few phone calls require a few moments of courage? Certainly. Were there nerves? Probably. Great lesson, though. Brief moments of courage can take your life to the next level quickly.

The Leap

I spent four hours in a church that afternoon. What on earth would I do? I think I knew this moment would come, but it was always someday. Creedence Clearwater Revival sings "Someday Never Comes" but in my life, that Friday was someday. Now what? It was a bit of a Matrix moment. Which pill? Go back to from whence you came or go forward into the rabbit hole, where nothing is predictable, where you don't even know if you can survive. That morning, my life as a corporate America employee had ended. The I-V consisting of a bi-weekly direct deposit, healthcare, 401k, accruing vacation hours had been yanked from my arm, leaving a wound that I wasn't sure I knew how to heal. I had, more or less, done the I-V yanking myself. A few weeks prior, Dominika, Ella (then just eighteen months old), and I had returned from a full month in Italy. We stayed with a friend who was playing professional baseball in Arezzo, a great city 45 miles east of Florence in the heart of Tuscany. Arezzo is within a few hours' drive of just about every breathtaking Tuscan town your taste buds, inner architecture and art buff, and world tourist can dream of. Assisi is just a ninety minute drive to the east. Cortona is less than an hour south. All easy day trips: San Gimignano, Sienna, Montepulciano, Montalcino, La Verna, Orvietto, Pitigliano, Anghiari, San Leo, San Marino, Grossetto, Gubbio, Lucca... I am literally becoming hungrier as I write the words. The decision to make the trip and the decision to unplug my I-V both absolutely met the significant progress significantly scary criteria for me at that time in life.

The trip to Italy was actually the 2nd of its type. Dominika and I spent a month there while she was pregnant with Ella. For our first Italian trip, my consulting schedule allowed this four week sojourn between projects.

It started when a great friend, Steve, whose motto for many years has been "Live the Big Life", casually asked if I would help coach Arezzo's developmental baseball team. Why not? What kind of time frame was he talking about, a week or two? Six months was his casual, yet firm and expectant reply. On what planet was Steve now living? Steve had been playing professional baseball in Italy and also coaching younger players for several years. The

> "Every man dies. Not every man really lives."
> ~ *Braveheart*

Italian vino and espresso must be affecting his ability to grasp reality. One does not go to Italy for 6 months. Not a normal person, anyway. Okay, Steve, could a month work? It wasn't the answer he was looking for, but he consented for this first trip. One month in Italy. There's the beginning of a vision for you! We could do that. Now Steve began asking when? When would our flight arrive? Well, actually booking a flight wasn't really what I had in mind. Somehow, I guess I must have thought that telling Steve we would come for a month and just leaving it at some undetermined month in the future might satisfy Steve's request.

I really don't know what I was thinking. Great dream and on that magical someday we would make it all happen! But Steve was quite committed to this idea of booking a flight. Even though I thought my schedule could somehow allow a month, I was certainly not ready to figure out exactly how to translate somehow and someday into a month on the real calendar, with paid-for airline tickets solidifying the whole thing.

"When? Live the big life! When?" Steve would ask.

"Okay, let me start pricing some airline tickets."

Was I delusional? Was I pricing tickets just to buy more time? Just pick two dates already. It's really that simple. But... No. It is that simple. I bought tickets. We were going. Now I had to figure out how to make this work. I won't pretend it was a piece of cake. Once the tickets were booked, Dominika and I were in a mad frenzy to figure out how to get our work schedules to allow this hiatus. Could we really afford this trip?

But, we did it. We did it. What an amazing trip. We toured so much of Italy. Rome, Pisa, La Cinque Terre, Verona, Florence, Venice, Assisi, Perugia, Cortona. I could go on and on. I helped coach baseball. My little brother, Peter, who was just 17 at the time, played for the Italian team in a baseball tournament. My niece, Olivia, just 7 years old then, fell head over heels for Gelato (pretty much any and all flavors) ... and Peter. The trip was full of lifelong memories! A lifetime of memories almost didn't happen. What made it happen? I finally put a stake in the ground. I have to say that I've shared versions of this story with a lot of people and, as a result, I have started to ask myself and others about putting stakes in the ground. When was the last time that you put a stake in the ground about something and then were not able to make it happen? Most people tell me that it's very rare. Once the stake is in the ground, it happens, regardless of what it might be. My next question: what stake do you need to put in the ground today?

Our second trip to Italy for a full month followed almost the exact same process. For round two, Steve was convinced that we should just make it 6 months. At that time, I wasn't willing to convince myself that this was possible. Yes, you read that right. I wasn't willing to convince myself that this was possible. Putting the stake in the ground for a one month return trip was easier. But, despite the lesson of the stake, I still resisted putting in a 6 month stake. We know, but we don't do. Putting a stake in the ground requires courage. In a culture that promotes

> **"He who is brave is free."**
> **~ Seneca**

instant gratification, putting stakes in the ground based on our real priorities is becoming an endangered species. It's time to start practicing this again.

During that second Italian trip, I kept asking what's next for my life. I knew that I wasn't in the sweet spot of overlapping my Talents and Passions to Serve. I was doing good work, using my talents, occasionally engaging my passions, but I knew that I wasn't serving the world at the level I was capable of. I spent many moments on hills in Italy, in churches, wandering through Assisi and La Verna, asking what Matthew Kelly calls the ultimate question: "God, what do you think I should do next?" For several years now, I have been convinced that when you are in line with your purpose, you will feel a sense of deep peace. That peace was accompanied with a decision to move on. To break my ties with my corporate job. To find ways to serve in a greater capacity. That question and its answer brought me to the beginning of this section. Sitting in a church on a Friday afternoon back in the US, just a few months after returning from Italy. I had ended my corporate America position, yanked the I-V out of my arm, without the next steps solidified. But it was time to drive that stake deep into the earth. I would find a way to serve at a greater level. Nervous? Yes. Scared? Yes. Feeling courageous? Sometimes.

Learning and practicing this new word

No. Would you like fries with that? No. Can you do an event on Mother's Day? No. Would you like some desert? Nnnnnnnn…. Great question. What do you have? Still practicing, expecting to get better over time. Maybe that's a lesson I need more frying pan experiences with before I am ready to learn!

I have to admit that there came a time when I started questioning how a person, a family, a company, a culture can thrive without the members intentionally building character. These traits feed off of each other with exponential impact. Without courage, you can't try to live within the three circles of clarity. Without the three circles, I wasn't likely to have the courage to say no to good in order to say yes to great. The business classic, *Good to Great*, starts with the sentence "Good is the enemy of great." As I discussed briefly in the three circles model, I started building a franchise with big green buses that didn't quite fit my model. Courage to say NO makes it possible to follow your clear vision. But here I was, now making my living from something outside of my vision. Sure, there were pieces of this adventure that touched on one or more of my circles. I was serving children and families, helping them fall in love with fitness, helping them build their own courage. However, gaining clarity that this business was not my whole life took my courageousness to the next level. I had unplugged the I-V, hammered into the ground that stake of serving at a deeper level. What would it mean if I settled? In gaining clarity of what I was built for, things I was busy doing needed to be done by someone else. I did not want to face the idea that I couldn't do everything. How do you say no to the good so that the great has room in your life? Courage. From where? Courage to say no springs from finding a bigger yes.

Saving Private Ryan is based on a true story, a story of an Iowa farm boy whose three brothers were all KIA, killed in action, during World War Two. The US military decided that Private James Ryan was not to share the fate of his brothers. A famous letter written by Abe Lincoln to Mrs. Bixby in Massachusetts mourning the loss of all five of her sons during the Civil War sets the stage for the attempt to find Private Ryan and bring him back home. Eight men champion the cause, led by Captain Miller, played by Tom Hanks. The attempts to find James Ryan take the group through war ravaged France and through several bloody skirmishes. In the end of the movie, Private Ryan's life has been saved and he'll be sent home, but not without tremendous cost. Most of the eight men sent to rescue the surviving brother have been killed and Captain Miller has been mortally wounded in the final battle scene. The captain looks Private Ryan in the eyes and utters his last words, "Earn this! Earn it!" The movie flashes forward to Private Ryan standing in Arlington National Cemetery at the cross with Captain Miller's name. Ryan utters to his wife, "Tell me I lived a good life."

For me, the courage to say no to good, to say no to things outside my unique overlap, springs from knowing that I've been given so much and that so many have sacrificed greatly. In the 20th century alone, 50 million citizens of our planet died on the altar of freedom. What if I wasted my short stay on this planet? What if I don't serve the world in the ways that only I am able? Viktor Frankl said, "Everyone has his own specific vocation or mission in life... therein he cannot be replaced, nor can his life be repeated..."

As each of the frying pan moments captured my attention, I slowly started to create an awareness that if I were to fulfill my unique mission, the word "no" would need to be applied to so many pretty good options. Does knowing that you have a unique

> "Courage is contagious. When a brave man takes a stand, the spines of others are often stiffened."
> ~ Billy Graham

mission scare you? Or energize you? Or both? I have to admit that I've certainly experienced both on more than one occasion since accepting the philosophy that I was built to serve the world in my unique manner. Leadership expert John Maxwell in *Put Your Dream to the Test* writes "I don't believe that God makes mistakes. He doesn't create people to be talented in one area but interested in an unrelated one." Joyce Meyer's similarly says, "God will help you be all you can be, but He will never help you be someone else."

I had known for a while that the big green bus was a good cause, but not the great cause for which I should spend my life. I had read Jim Collins' book, Good to Great, several times and the first sentence was etched into my mind. "Good is the enemy of great." How does that make sense? Often we arrive at good and stop searching for great. Good pizza places are a simple example. How many good pizza places exist within twenty miles of your home? Probably dozens, maybe even more. How many great pizza places are in that same radius?

My green bus business was a good thing. The business was doing well (or as our culture likes to say "we're doin' pretty gooooood!"). We were actually the #1 franchise within the system for three consecutive years. Pretty good, indeed. But are good and great enemies? Well, I had become somewhat comfortable. Ray Kroc, the visionary leader who built McDonald's into the largest restaurant chain and real estate holder in the world, put it best: "Either you're green and growing or ripe and rotting!" I guess I was ripe and rotting, but I had really known and ignored this for quite some time. I had decided that it was time to move on several years ago, but the green bus was still a distraction from a vision that was becoming more and more clear. I was supposed to use my talents and passions to serve. I was supposed to speak and teach, to challenge myself, and then others, to become. It came naturally, gave me energy, kept me up at night, but I still was only doing it now and then. The bus had to go, literally!

I've seen this lesson repeated by leaders. The lesson is addressed twice, and both times unbelievably well, in the movie, *Troy*. In the beginning of the movie, Achilles is sought to fight a battle against one of the most immense human beings on the planet. The boy who delivers the message tells Achilles, "...he's the biggest man I've ever seen. I wouldn't want to fight him." Achilles' cold response: "That's why no one will remember your name."

I started to think that I might have to watch that scene repeatedly for a few weeks until I got the point. If I don't start saying no to good in order to make room for great, no one will remember my name. Not that people remembering my name is the goal, but making a difference certainly is. I changed the line in my mind to "Lives you are supposed to touch won't be impacted" Later in the movie, Achilles' protégé, Petrocles is killed in battle. Achilles rides off to the wall of Troy to avenge this loss. He calls out "HECTOR! HECTOR!" - calling for the prince of Troy to meet him in battle. At this point in history, wars would occasionally be settled in this manner. The two cities, nations, or

> "To avoid criticism say nothing, do nothing, be nothing."
> ~ Aristotle

armies would settle the battle by pitting the champions from each side against each other in a winner-take-all fight. Achilles was challenging Hector to such a battle. How many times would I know what battle had to be fought, what bold step should be next or what good thing had to be turned down, in order to make tremendous progress in life? As purpose becomes clearer, the Hectors in our lives become the major distractions from that purpose. Even though I had known this for some time, I wasn't ready to go to my wall of Troy and call it out. What are the Hectors in your life right now? For some, it is setting time aside to create clarity of vision. For others, it is exercising the courage to take action towards that vision. I've had times in my life when the Hector was Applied Teach-ability, actually becoming humble enough to both learn a lesson and apply it. It could be forgiving someone, including yourself for past mistakes or failures. Pick one Hector and rout it out of your life. As Thoreau wrote over 160 years ago, "I went to the woods because I wished to live deliberately, to front only the essential facts of life, and see if I could not learn what it had to teach, and not, when I came to die, discover that I had not lived. I did not wish to live what was not life, living is so dear... I wanted to live deep and suck out all the marrow of life ... to put to rout all that was not life..."

No problem IS a problem

During an automotive consulting project, I had the chance to work with a team from the Toyota Cambridge engine plant. This Canadian facility was renowned for winning repeated quality awards. The team shared a great story about a meeting with their plant manager just after winning yet another prestigious quality award. The managers were celebrating and in very high spirits when the plant manager asked what the problems were. The team responded with a quizzical look and confidently stated, "We have no problems." Their wise plant manager's reply: "No problems means no need for managers." He had taught them that their primary role as leaders was to demonstrate and teach a tool that management circles know as PDCA. Plan, Do, Check, Adjust. Find challenges, then make a plan to affect them, do (execute) the plan, check progress, adjust the plan, and repeat until the problem is solved. After putting together the lessons from Troy and the Toyota Cambridge team, I realized that most of us plateau in life, in business, as parents, as families, as leaders, as friends… because we fail to PDCA around one significant Hector at a time. Write down the Hectors that are currently holding you back. Evaluate the significance of each, perhaps estimating the number of lives that you won't be able to positively impact this year if you don't address each specific Hector. Pick one Hector and PDCA.

A few examples:
    Listening
    Actually caring for the people you lead
    Holding yourself &/or your team accountable
    Forgiving
    Building confidence
    Trusting
    Hiring people more capable than you
    Starting that business
    Closing that business

Going back to school
Becoming a person of Integrity
Being fully present with those around you
Fixing that relationship
Owning your attitude
Getting to know your Maker
Trusting your Abilities

PDCA is just an expanded version of Focus and Feedback. Pick one Hector and take it on. A few months from now, a year from now, your life and your impact on others will be at another level.

World Class Family

Emotional Intelligence is on a rapid decline in modern civilization. Many studies agree that two of the leading causes are decaying family life and lack of spirituality. Children grow up feeling as if there is no safe place - no place they can go where they are totally and unconditionally loved and accepted. The family unit, if it's even still intact, has little time for childhood. TV, video games, music, the internet own more and more of our children's attention. Over the course of a young child's formative first decade, the average child's time in contact with the media, babysitters, daycares, and preschools dwarfs the amount of time spent with parents. Spirituality has been questioned and church attendance throughout most of Europe and the United States is on a dramatic decline. Without belief in a higher power or a higher purpose, children start to believe that their challenges are too big to be handled. If this weren't enough, divorce tears another rip in our children's emotional state.

What if you wanted to build a world class family? Where might you find an example? Author Matthew Kelly writes that you can predict the direction of a nation by looking at the story tellers. Who are the story tellers and what story are they telling? The thoughts and actions of a people follow the stories that the people focus on. Our story tellers are telling

> "You don't choose your family. They are God's gift to you, as you are to them."
> ~ Desmond Tutu

a story of broken marriages, miserable marriages, deceitful marriages, reckless parents. What primetime television show tells the story of a world class family today? Once upon a time Aesop's Fables were the stories of a great nation. Children grew up trying to live up to those ideals. Today, our story tellers rarely point out ideals that are worth living up to. Or we allow the famous to become the storytellers, regardless of their story. A few years ago I began thinking about the concept of a world class family. What courageous acts must a world class family perform? No cable TV. I don't know if that's a must, but we've not had cable TV in my home now for 4 years. Dinner together as a family on a regular basis. Turn down some of the birthday party invites my daughters get because we have scheduled family time. I need to have the courage to be a great husband and father. Sometimes that means loving my family enough to give them what they need, but might not necessarily want. Many times it means being open to, and even seeking feedback from my wife. I joke in seminars about getting feedback from your spouse by using a simple question, "Honey, on a scale of 1 to 10, how am I doing as a spouse? And if it's not a 10, what would make it a 10?" To which the spouse might just respond, "You're a 2 out of 10. Stop asking dumb questions and you might just move up a few points." Simple questions that might take some courage to ask include what could I do to be a better husband this week or what is one change I could make that would have a radical impact on our relationship?

One thing I believe about families with absolute certainty: we need more parents to decide that they will pursue a world-class marriage and family life. Not just decide, but dedicate time and energy each day to keeping this focus and building a family life that supports this vision

Chapter 5

Happen to the World

Mother Male was just a little bit different from all the other teachers I had ever experienced. She was our 7th grade science teacher and that could be one challenging role. We all just stared at her with that world famous blank, why are you trying so hard to convince us that we want to learn this look on our faces as Mrs. Male explained to us that we shall refer to her as Mother Male. Apparently she had been teaching since before any of us were born, so we assumed the Mother reference might pertain to her as the Mother of Time. Mother Male had learned a few things in her time and was about to teach a lesson that I am finally beginning to understand. Standing in the front of the classroom on that winter morning, Mrs. Male casually mentioned that we would be learning the classification system for living organisms. If there is something more exciting to a 12- or 13-year-old, I still have yet to discover it. We were practically sitting on the edges of our seats to hear about this blend of Latin and English. Somehow, Mother Male understood our state of apathy, paused, stared us down, and seemed to calculate some plan, all within a split second. Like an improv actress, she flashed into ready mode and began a solo chant:

"Kingdom…..
   Phylum – Class – Order …
   Family – Genus – Species.
     Phylum – Class – Order …
     Family – Genus – Species."

As Mother Male chanted, she began to dance around the front of our classroom, punctuating each word with an arm, leg, head, or body gesture. Most of the class simply stared, mesmerized. Those of us in the class still capable of conscious thought were beginning to think that Mother Male had truly outdone herself, and that we may not see her any more. Any in doubt of this were convinced immediately when Mother Male stopped her dancing and chanting routine abruptly, spun towards the class, and excitedly announced that we might all just want to stand up and join her in the routine. She had clearly lost it. Poor Mother Male. She always meant well, but our older siblings' classes must have worn her down. Begrudgingly, we all stood up and performed the 7th grade cool person dance chant, dancing with as little of our bodies as possible involved in any movement. It took some serious determination from Mother Male, but after a few minutes, she had the group chanting and dancing along. Thinking Mrs. Male had gone as far as she could was, we would soon realize, a gross miscalculation. A sudden pause in the chant and a look of wild excitement in her eyes as if she had just discovered fire got us all to freeze. "Congo Line!" We were now dancing, chanting, and parading up and down the classroom aisles "Kingdom... Phylum Class Order .. Family Genus Species" accentuating every word with an arm, leg, or head gesture. We were somehow freed from our 7th grade inhibitions momentarily, caught up in the rhythm of the Latin/English chant Congo line. A few weeks later, test day arrived. One of the questions asked us to name the classification system for living organisms. Heads started to bop around the classroom. We were like dominos. One head, then a few more, finally all bouncing simultaneously. Several classmates even incorporated

body movements. Humming "Kingdom… Phylum Class Order."
How many students got that question wrong? Oh, I don't think
any of us. In fact, you could likely track down my whole 7th grade
class today and they'd dance-chant the answer for you. What
exactly did Mother Male do? She understood one of the most
important lessons of the 20th century. Let me share it in a simple
three letter formula that our teacher had mastered.

$$S + R = O$$

Situation + Response = Outcome

Our teacher wanted a certain outcome (O) - us to learn the
material, which for simplicity's sake can be translated into getting
an A on the test or a 4 out of a possible 4. From her perspective,
the students were part of the Situation, or S, part of the formula.
She knew that a group of 7th graders might not bring all 4 points
to the equation to garner the A. Many of us might bring closer to
a 0 or 1. With this understanding, Mother Male changed the part
of the equation that she had complete control over, her
response, the R. Her R contributed all 4 points required to get
the whole class to 4, unless we didn't show up for class that day.
Flipping the scenario around, I think we've all had a teacher that
didn't do what Mrs. Male did. From our perspective that teacher
is part of the S and may have contributed close to 0 in the
formula. That leaves you and I to respond with a 4 if we want the
outcome to be 4. Too many in our culture today point at the
situation (S), thus abdicating responsibility for the final outcome.
History may come to define our age as the age of abdication of
responsibility. If I spill hot coffee on my lap, it must be the fault

of the situation, the café that made the coffee so hot, the car company that didn't put enough cup holders in my car, or the radio station that played a song that made me dance as I dropped the hot coffee on my lap. We all need to join my 7th grade science teacher in understanding and living this simple equation a little bit better! Mother Male happened to the world, rather than letting the world happen to her.

Our language abdicates responsibility

"She made me so mad!" Ella announced to Mom and Dad, with tears forming in her eyes. One look at her face and any parent could instantly tell that she was not our happy little princess at that moment. Mad was just the tip of the iceberg. Furious

> "Let us not seek to fix the blame for the past. Let us accept our own responsibility for the future."
> ~ John F. Kennedy

might be a better word. But – and this is a pretty big but – did her friend really make her mad? If not, who had made our perfect little angel so unhappy?

> *"How do you think that made him feel?"*
> *"That customer really aggravated me!"*
> *"Every time my boss does that, it drives me insane!"*
> *"The economy is killing us."*
> *"The referees cost us the game. You can't win 7 on 5."*

I don't think I'm the only one in our culture that has used these expressions to abdicate responsibility for my results, outcome, business, emotional state, or life. That sentence may sound harsh, but it can start all too easily. I played sports constantly growing up; baseball, basketball, soccer, volleyball, hockey. So many referees and umpires cost me a game, or so my language at the time would have led you and me to believe. Even as adults, so often we hear people in the stands complain at a sporting event that the officials are losing the game for our team. This mindset and philosophy wouldn't gain any ground if it were directly introduced. Instead, it seeps into our world, through a seemingly harmless phrase here or there, until it has a hold on our world view. When my words give someone else control over my emotional state, the tendency is for that control to swell into control over my entire life. Come on, Jonathan, you're being just a bit dramatic. Oh really? Am I? Let me give a very simple example of something that happens every single day in our country. I was in Atlanta presenting a workshop on "BECOMING a Creative Leader: Lessons from Walt Disney" and the day was going great. The group was very engaged, had tremendous questions and examples, and translated ideas into workable approaches for their specific reality. At lunch time, however, I typically get feedback from a group, often in written form so that all can share their thoughts and it can remain anonymous. The most frequent recommended improvement from that group: raise the temperature in the room. Now, my wife might tell you that I can be temperature impaired at times. I am warm-blooded and rarely cold when speaking in front of an audience. These participants sat in that room for the whole morning feeling a bit too cold without saying a word about it and without walking over to the thermostat and raising the temperature a few degrees. I smiled as big as I could and said, "You're allowed to fix the temperature." The participants were all leaders in their businesses and the whole seminar was about leadership and creativity. It reminds me of a great saying that you may have heard. Finish it for me: "An apple a day…" You know the ending, right? "An apple a day keeps the doctor away." What if that were true? I am still searching for the person that follows that wisdom. My wife and I put a lot of focus into helping our children understand a similarly wise expression that we want each member of our family to live by. I am in charge of me. Ella is in charge of Ella. Dadda is in charge of Dadda. Mama is in charge of Mama. No one else gets to decide our emotional response to anything. Nobody can make you mad. As Eleanor Roosevelt said, "Nobody can make you feel inferior without your consent." You may think I'm a little too much on this one, but I try to catch every phrase that I say or anyone in my family says that gives up that ability to choose our own responses to the world.

$S + R = O.$

Does the economy affect my business? Of course. That's part of the "S" or situation. The economy does not, however, control the rest of the equation. Does Ella's friend do things that Ella might not like? Of course. But if the friend makes Ella mad, that's giving up the rest of the formula.

> "The price of greatness is responsibility"
> ~ Winston Churchill

As I mentioned earlier, for the past several years, every occasion that warrants a child getting gifts, birthday, Christmas, Hanukkah, we have given each child in our life two books; Sean Covey's Seven Habits of Happy Kids and Matthew Kelly's Why am I Here? Sammy Squirrel, the chapter 1 star of Covey's book teaches that Sammy is in charge of Sammy. Ella gets that now. What if all six-year-olds got that? How different would the world be? What if all adults got it? That's just crazy talk. If the stories we know become the lives we lead, what stories will you make sure your children learn?

We are born into the World
Like a blank canvas
And every person that crosses our path
Takes up the brush
And makes their mark
Upon our surface.
So it is that we develop.
But we must realize there comes a day
That we must take up the brush
And finish the work.
For only we can determine
If we are to be
Just another painting
Or a Masterpiece

~ Javen

Who are you becoming?

Will you become a masterpiece? Become YOU.

The Unknown town of Oswiecim

I met my wife's grandparents on my first trip to Poland in 1996. They were two of the most pure, kind-hearted people I have ever met. Without understanding more than a few dozen words in Polish at that time, I was still able to connect with Babcia and Djaju. He was a solid man, probably about six feet tall and built to move the earth. When I first shook his hand, I realized in an instant that his might be the largest hands I had ever seen. Yet these hands were somehow the combination of strength, capability, and gentleness. When he told me with quite a bit of translation assistance to take care of his granddaughter, I knew he meant it. This couple had lived off the land, through their hard work, patience, dedication, will, and humility. They had also lived through one of the greatest tragedies of human history. The Nazi forces invaded Poland without warning on September 1, 1939 and steamrolled through the unprepared nation. Concentration work camps were established rather quickly and the first prisoners to occupy these camps in Poland were the key influencers in the country. Prisoners include mayors, business people, religious leaders, and active community members. Anyone that the Nazi machine thought might organize any type of resistance was rounded up. Statues of historic figures and historic sites were obliterated, because this terribly effective propaganda machine understood a simple fact of human nature: if we get rid of heroes and a connection to the past, we can radically affect the identity of a people. The truth of that sentence scares me today. We, as a culture, seem to be getting rid of heroes on our own, without the assistance of a totalitarian dictator. We look for holes in every hero's armor, almost wanting to get rid of any example of excellence that might make us uncomfortable. What happened to the wise words of Ralph Waldo Emerson, "Every man I meet is in some way my superior; and in that I can learn of him." After rounding up the living and destroying the past Polish influencers, the Nazis began to turn the work camps into death camps for what would be known to the Nazi party as the "Final Solution" and to the world as the Holocaust. My wife's grand-parents, these two kind, gentle, strong people that welcomed me into their home had experienced this horror first hand. They lived in a farming town of Przemysl, east of Krakow by about 120 miles and close to the

WW2 Russian border. Most of my communication with Dominika's grandparents was in their limited German, which they had learned in order to survive during the Nazi occupation. Grandpa explained to me that he hid Jewish people in the basement of his home during this time. My first thought was "of course, who wouldn't do that to help save lives?" Then grandpa explained that any person found to be hiding Jews would not just be punished personally. Their whole extended family, spouse, children, cousins, parents, aunts and uncles, nieces and nephews would be rounded up and taken to a "Final Solution" extermination camp. As a result, this fostered an environment where a nephew whose uncle was harboring Jews might inform the Nazi party in order to spare his own life. Despite the potential cost, Dominika's grandparents did what was right, what they felt was the only option. In my conversations with them, I got the impression that there was never a question, never a hesitation. They didn't even know the people that they hid, but knew what was right and put the lives of their entire family on the line for this. Through many trips to Poland and some research, I learned that Poland had one of the highest Jewish populations of the entire world, about 3.5 Million, before September 1, 1939. Today's Jewish population in Poland is roughly 3.5 Thousand. Yes, just 3,500. Perhaps you are familiar with Spielberg's film, Schindler's List? The descendants of the Schindler's List Jews outnumber the total current Polish Jew population by more than 2 to 1. Throughout history, so many who have given in to terror and ghastly regimes have said something like this: "under those circumstances, what else could we have done." My wife's grandparents might have used the Polish equivalent of this expression, but with the opposite intent. Under their circumstances, they saw helping, serving, laying down their own personal interests, sharing their limited food, risking the lives of all they held dear, for another person's life as the only choice.

August 28th, 1963 is a date that leaps from the pages of history books. Martin Luther King, Jr. delivered the "I have a dream" speech from the steps of the Lincoln Memorial. At that same podium, just before MLK's famous words, another speech was delivered. The speaker was a Jewish rabbi who had been exiled from Berlin in 1937 for doing precisely what he would challenge the American people to do on that 1963 summer day. King would remember this rabbi's message and quote it for the rest of his life. Rabbi Joachim Prinz shared this message and challenge:

"When I was the rabbi of the Jewish community in Berlin under the Hitler regime, I learned many things. The most important thing that I learned under those tragic circumstances was that bigotry and hatred are not the most urgent problem. The most urgent, the most disgraceful, the most shameful and the most tragic problem is silence.

A great people which had created a great civilization had become a nation of silent onlookers. They remained silent in the face of hate, in the face of brutality and in the face of mass murder.

America must not become a nation of onlookers. America must not remain silent."

This brings me to one of the greatest lessons of the 20th century, one whose story comes from an overlap of a Russian psychologist, some dogs, a German philosopher, an Austrian psychologist, and a town on the other side of Krakow. The Russian and his dogs lay the foundation for this lesson, so let's start with their side of the story. Pavlov's idea of classical conditioning is a simple concept and took the psychology world by storm. High school and college students throughout the

> "I recommend that the Statue of Liberty on the East Coast be supplemented by a Statue of Responsibility on the West Coast... If freedom is to endure, liberty must be joined with responsibility."
> ~ Viktor Frankl

world still learn about this famous experiment. Pavlov would ring a bell and then feed the dogs. The process of bell ringing and presenting food was repeated until the dogs linked bell to food. Pavlov would then ring the bell and observe the dogs beginning to salivate, in anticipation of what the bell now meant in their brain circuitry. Classical conditioning was born. Link a stimulus with a response. When A happens, I respond with B. The world loved this simple formula. Simple formulas that the world adopts can be very dangerous if the formula is flawed. This is where our German philosopher enters the picture. Friedrich Nietzsche rose to immense popularity in the late 1800s and early 1900s. His predominant philosophy was something I had come across in the final semester of my senior year in college, as part of a course that I had expected to be an easy A, an elective to simply fill a spot. This easy A turned into one of the most challenging courses of my college career. The course: Culture and Tyranny. Our study: how the Third Reich and the culture of early twentieth century Germany both fed into a spiral that became one of mankind's most horrific moments in history. Nietzsche's role was critical. Like all philosophers and scientists, he borrowed ideas from those who came before, a necessary process in development of sciences, but one that carries potential inherent danger. One of these great dangers that arises from borrowing ideas of one's predecessors can be seen quite graphically in the famous leaning tower of Pisa. The tower was built up, one row of brick on top of the row that came before. However, the tower leans at a 5.5 degree angle. Visitors to the top of the tower look down from one side to see that it is almost 15 feet away from the base 182 feet below. The lesson is simple. If one of the layers that you build upon is off, each subsequent layer will likely be off, with the error being magnified over time. Nietzsche had built on one of the most famous scientists of the 19th century, Charles Darwin. Darwin brought the world evolutionary theory and the phrase "survival of the fittest." Nietzsche built on top of this theory and many of his readers made two fatal assumptions:

- "God is dead." Many have added the phrase, "... and with Him die all sinners."
- Human evolution towards the "superman" (or ubermensch)

In order for humanity to keep evolving, some of humanity (under-men or untermensch) must go under. Adolf Hitler is said to have personally introduced the works of Nietzsche to Stalin and Mussolini in order to share and spread this philosophy. Am I saying that evolution is a flawed theory? No. I am saying that many interpreted Nietzsche, building on a crooked edge of evolution with the assumption that evolution precludes the existence of God and that survival of the fittest permits extermination of those deemed (under whose discretion?) to be less fit.

While either Pavlov or Nietzsche's philosophies, especially taken out of context, contain substantial danger, what are the ramifications of combining classical conditioning (stimulus creates response, or my environment creates me) with "God is dead" and facilitating human evolution?

These two theories set the stage for one of the 20th century's greatest lessons. Viktor Frankl lived an experience that turned this simple classical conditioning philosophy completely upside down. Born in Austria to Jewish parents, Frankl studied psychiatry and practiced as a determinist, following the Freud and Pavlov in the idea that what happens to you in your childhood determines the rest of your life. During the war, Frankl was imprisoned in death camps, including about a week spent in the once relatively unknown town of Ocwiecim, 150 miles west of Krakow, now known to the world as Auschwitz. Viktor Frankl's parents, wife, and brother all died in the camps. Through this experience, outlined in tremendous detail in Frankl's book, *Man's Search for Meaning*, Frankl came to understand what he would call the "last of human freedoms." We are able to choose our response despite the circumstances. My rough translation as this applies to Pavlov: "People are not dogs." If I walked around your neighborhood with a bell and a giant box of cookies, ringing the bell and doling out delicious cookies, you might come to expect your favorite cookies every time you saw me or heard my bell. But if I came through without the box of cookies one day, you would still retain this last of human freedoms, you could decide not to attack me screaming "Cookies, cookies, where are my cookies?" Frankl wrote about prisoners in his building that would give up hope. After experiencing this several times, he was often able to see hope fading in the eyes of a fellow inmate and he knew that it would then be only a matter of days or weeks before that person's loss of hope would deteriorate to the point of death, and that person would simply not get out of his bunk one morning. Frankl made it part of his mission to try to breathe hope back into those imprisoned with him. Ironically, the most common phrase repeated in *Man's Search for Meaning* is also from Friedrich Nietzsche, but quite contrary to the two concepts discussed earlier. The phrase: "He who has a *why* to live can bear with almost any *how*." Frankl created two driving reasons to survive this indescribable "how" of the camps. First, he would have imagined conversations with his wife on a regular basis. After being taken to the camps, they would never again see each other. However, Frankl would imagine that they were together some years after this was all over and they were discussing something together, perhaps dinner or plans for a vacation or upcoming holiday. His wife became one of his "Why's." The second, which he would often employ even while being tortured, was teaching the world the lessons he had learned from this experience. He might imagine himself in front of an audience explaining this last of human freedoms, this ability to choose one's response despite the circumstances while he was being beaten by the guards. Many years after the war, Viktor Frankl was invited to speak to the United Nations in NYC. A key to his speech that the entire world should etch in stone above schools, government buildings, homes, playgrounds, on highways: "I recommend that the Statue of Liberty on the East Coast be supplemented by a Statue of Responsibility on the West Coast... If freedom is to endure, liberty must be joined with responsibility."

My trip from my wife's grandparents' village to this once obscure town west of Krakow took about 5 hours. My wife's cousin and I chatted here and there, but spent most of the journey in an uncomfortable silence. This was just a foreshadowing of one of the most influential experiences of my life. As we approached our destination, a heaviness began to overwhelm my whole being. I hadn't done a great deal of research about the town before the trip, but seemed to know enough to feel completely oppressed. Ordinarily, I am energized by touching history, but this was different. Very different. Ocwiecim is the Polish word for Auschwitz, the most efficient human killing factory in world history. This killing machine took the lives of somewhere between 1 and 1.5 Million people in less than 5 years, increasing its capabilities to the point that 10,000 lives could be exterminated in one day.

Full trainloads containing thousands of people could be taken off of the two sets of tracks, routed directly into the two main gas chambers at the end of the tracks, and two thousand people in the basement of each crematorium were murdered, gassed with Zyklon-B. These main crematoriums were demolished just before the war ended by the Nazis, in attempts to hide their war crimes. The basements of each still remain. An overwhelming state of sorrow, anger, sadness, and despair seems to completely envelop the entire site. I stood inside boarding houses, where hundreds of laborers would be housed. I touched the bunk spaces, boxes about 6 feet by 6 feet by 6 feet, where as many as 15 prisoners would sleep each night, in three neat rows of five. Next to the two sets of train tracks, prisoners had been forced to dig steep trenches, so any prisoner who tried to run upon arrival would get to the bottom of a trench, struggle to climb out, and be shot. I went into a trench to feel the helplessness of one who might have tried to escape. Panic overtook me. By the time I climbed out, tears were pouring down my cheeks. Many of the buildings are now turned into exhibits to tell this horrific story. One massive room is divided in half by long glass panels. As you walk along the glass, you see 5,000 pounds of human hair, all found with traces of the killing gas, Zyklon-B, contracts to sell the hair to weavers, and a selection of products made from human hair, including rugs, curtains, shirts. Not a word is spoken in most of the rooms. Tears flow freely. I couldn't tell if I was close to vomiting or fainting. Another room is full of shoes taken from the men and women before they were gassed. Yet another room has evidence of the ghastly experiments conducted on prisoners, primarily young children, with a special focus on twins. A room full of items that bring smiles and laughter in almost any circumstance proved to be one of the most debilitating exhibits for many visitors. The room was full of children's toys and clothing. Roughly 300,000 children entered Auschwitz. Less than 300 left. When I entered the chamber where the first gassing with Zyklon-B was conducted, a facility still very much intact, my body froze as I looked up to the shafts in the roof, through which the canisters of the gas pellets were poured. My body quivered. To this day, I don't know which image horrified me more, that of the murdered victims and their families, or imagining the murderers and how they could possibly commit such acts. Nietzsche's words and accompanying assumption, "God is dead, [and with Him die all sinners]" became a resounding gong, pounding on my head. With no standard, somehow did these people believe that they were assisting the process of survival of the fittest? I have seen mean people. I have not always been the perfect neighbor to the world. But getting so close to this experience, I could not fathom how it happened. How high up this leaning tower had these cold-blooded mass-murderers climbed? Now I was starting to understand Socrates' willingness to lay down his life rather than lead the unexamined life. If we don't examine the foundations upon which our lives as individuals, families, communities, cultures, nations, and the world are built, may George Santayana's world famous quote carved in Auschwitz in Polish and English serve as our warning:

"Kto nie pamieta historii skazany jest na jej ponowne przezycie."

"The one who does not remember history is bound to live through it again."

My visit to Auschwitz is one of the primary reasons for writing this book. You and I need to start really looking at the philosophies that drive our lives. We could all too easily say that the culture or the media or the schools or the world does all these things to us, but that would be missing Viktor Frankl's whole point. You and I each have that last of the human freedoms. We get to choose our response to the world. It starts with stepping back to see what philosophies have been guiding our lives and evaluating the fruits of these philosophies. It's time to bring questions like "Who am I BECOMING? Who am I helping those around me to BECOME?" into a central role in our lives.

"I could only thank him with my eyes."

It was a sunny day in May, but nothing about the day felt like spring. This day would be a reminder of death. A reminder of a deep sadness. A reminder of tragedy and the horrors of which mankind is capable. In the midst of all this, one man's sacrifice brought hope and proof that light exists. That good exists. That love exists.

I nearly collapsed standing at the entrance to the starvation bunker cell for the "Saint of Auschwitz", and I was moved to learn more about this man. How did he have the courage to make that ultimate decision?

Raymond Kolbe was born on January 8th, 1894 Zduńska Wola, in central Poland, and was a man ahead of his time. One day, after this mischievous child had been up to his usual trouble, his mother asked Raymond what was to become of him. Very shortly thereafter, a vision of the Virgin Mary had a profound impact on Raymond's life.

As he described the vision:

"... the Mother of God.... came to me holding two crowns, one white, the other red. She asked me if I was willing to accept either of these crowns. The white one meant that I should persevere in purity, and the red that I should become a martyr. I said that I would accept them both."

At just sixteen years of age, he dedicated his life to his faith, entering a Franciscan seminary. Raymond changed his name to Maximilian Maria Kolbe, founded a newspaper, which would become Poland's top seller at over 1,000,000 copies in circulation by the 1930's, leveraged radio to help spread his message, founded and built a monastery near Warsaw which would become the largest monastery in the world during Kolbe's lifetime and another monastery in Nagasaki, Japan. Kolbe built the Nagasaki monastery in the 1930's on the far side of a mountain, and had he followed Japanese Shinto beliefs, he would have built on the opposite side of the mountain, which was obliterated by the atomic bomb dropped there just a decade later.

Back in Poland in 1941, Kolbe was imprisoned by the Nazis and transported to Auschwitz as prisoner #16670 on May 28th. Kolbe's crime: his Polish monastery was hiding 2,000 Jews to protect them from the regime that had taken over his country. Auschwitz in its early days was primarily used as a work camp and camp for enemies of the Nazi state. The prisoners that survived did so on about half of today's recommended USDA calorie count, often a cup of imitation coffee serving as breakfast and

> "The real conflict is the inner conflict. Beyond armies of occupation and the hecatombs of extermination camps, there are two irreconcilable enemies in the depth of every soul: good and evil, sin and love. And what use are the victories on the battlefield if we ourselves are defeated in our innermost personal selves?"
> ~ Saint Maximilian Kolbe

weak soup with a half loaf of bread after work, scarcely enough to sustain a young child. Most prisoners clamored for their place in line when food was brought. Kolbe waited until all were fed and often nothing was left for him. When he did get a portion, he would share this meager ration with other inmates.

He rarely slept, making rounds within the cell, stopping at each bunk saying, "I am a Catholic priest. Can I do anything for you?" One of the surviving prisoners later recalled crawling across the floor with other inmates to be near Father Kolbe's bunk. Kolbe encouraged his fellow prisoners to overcome evil with good, and to choose to forgive their captors. When being beaten by the guards, this man chose to pray for his persecutors rather than scream out. In order to prevent attempted escape plans, Auschwitz had a policy that any escapee from a bunker would be punished by the murder of 10 from that same bunker.

In the end of July 1941, a prisoner had disappeared from Kolbe's bunker, so the prison commander gathered all the prisoners and selected ten to be starved and dehydrated to death in underground cells in order to prevent future escape attempts. "My wife! My children! What will they do?" cried out Franciszek Gajowniczek, one of the young men selected.

Tadeusz Raznikiewicz, an Auschwitz survivor who lived in Sweden after the war, was standing in line that day. Tadeusz had been taken to the camp because Nazi soldiers found him after curfew with a copy of an underground newspaper within which was an article written by a former Auschwitz inmate. This article was the first public appearance of any news coming from inside witnesses of this death camp. Raznikiewicz describes a mass that Father Kolbe held a few days before this fateful day in secret in Auschwitz Block 14. He knew of Father Kolbe before entering Auschwitz from the work that he had done with the publication, radio, monastery, and his Japanese mission. Tadeusz said the intention of the ten prisoners being starved and dehydrated was simple. The promise was that if the escapee returned, the ten would be released. This had never happened.

As the entire block of about 400 men was lined up, Tadeusz was in the fourth row, while Kolbe was in the fifth row, diagonally behind Tadeusz. Announcement was made that ten would be selected, locked up, and be given absolutely no food or water. They would die of lack of water. One man was selected at a time, as the Lagerfuhrer walked slowly up and down the line, looking each man in the eyes as he passed, deciding which to send to their death. A very thin and very suntanned man, probably from working under the hot sun, according to Tadeusz, was selected. This man, Franciszek, was forcibly pulled from the line by two guards. The line of ten had been chosen. The prisoners stood shoulder to shoulder and an eerie deathly silence overtook them.

Tadeusz felt a push from behind, as someone was breaking ranks, pushing himself through the line. Father Kolbe stepped forward, removing his hat.

"Was ist los? Was ist los?" [What is the matter?] came from the Lagerfuhrer.

Kolbe replied softly, "I am a Catholic priest. Let me take his place. I am old. He has a wife and children."

"Bist du verruckt?" [Are you crazy?]

Witnesses were petrified. They knew that Kolbe's request could easily be taken as a challenge to authority and both men might die as a result. Instead, the Nazi commander allowed the swap, perhaps noting that the older priest might be less useful in the work camp than the younger Gajowniczek, who later recalled:

"I could only thank him with my eyes. I was stunned and could hardly grasp what was going on. The immensity of it: I, the condemned, am to live and someone else willingly and voluntarily offers his life for me - a stranger. Is this some dream?
I was put back into my place without having had time to say anything to Maximilian Kolbe. I was saved. And I owe to him the fact that I could tell you all this. The news quickly spread all round the camp. It was the first and the last time that such an incident happened in the whole history of Auschwitz.

For a long time I felt remorse when I thought of Maximilian. By allowing myself to be saved, I had signed his death warrant. But now, on reflection, I understood that a man like him could not have done otherwise. Perhaps he thought that as a priest his place was beside the condemned men to help them keep hope. In fact he was with them to the last."

Hundreds of men watched in deathly silence as the two men traded places.

Instead of tears and screaming from these ten men, recitation of the rosary prayer and hymns came from this death block, Block 13. Kolbe was often found kneeling in his cell and with a calm serenity to his figure. He outlived the other nine prisoners who were sentenced to death that day. Execution by starvation and dehydration was the order. Within a few days, the brains of those prisoners would feel on fire from lack of fluids.

Bruno Borgowiec, a Polish prisoner assigned to working the starvation bunker in the basement of Building 13 shared this with his parish priest shortly after the war:

"The ten condemned to death went through terrible days. From the underground cell in which they were shut up there continually arose the echo of prayers and canticles. The man in-charge of emptying the buckets of urine found them always empty. Thirst drove the prisoners to drink the contents. Since they had grown very weak, prayers were now only whispered. At every inspection, when almost all the others were now lying on the floor, Father Kolbe was seen kneeling or standing in the center as he looked cheerfully in the face of the SS men.

Father Kolbe never asked for anything and did not complain, rather he encouraged the others, saying that the fugitive might be found and then they would all be freed. One of the SS guards remarked: this priest is really a great man. We have never seen anyone like him ...

Two weeks passed in this way. Meanwhile one after another they died, until only Father Kolbe was left. The "Saint of Auschwitz" had outlasted the authorities' patience. The cell was needed for new victims. So one day they brought in the head of the sick-quarters, a German named Bock, who gave Father Kolbe an injection of carbolic acid in the vein of his left arm. Father Kolbe, with a prayer on his lips, himself gave his arm to the executioner. Unable to watch this I left under the pretext of work to be done. Immediately after the SS men had left I returned to the cell, where I found Father Kolbe leaning in a sitting position against the back wall with his eyes open and his head drooping sideways. His face was calm and radiant..."

And so the Saint of Auschwitz passed from this life. That was August 14th. Kolbe's body was cremated the next day, on the Catholic Feast day of the Assumption of Mary, the Mother of God, to whom Maximilian Maria Kolbe had dedicated his life. Auschwitz survivor Jerzy Bielecki described Father Kolbe's death as "a shock filled with hope, bringing new life and strength ... It was like a powerful shaft of light in the darkness of the camp."

But what would become of Franciszek, the young father whose life Kolbe had spared? Each year for the remaining of his 95 years on earth, on August 14th, this man would return to Auschwitz to honor the man who had died on his behalf. He did reunite with his wife, but both of his sons were killed during the war. Gajowniczek was in attendance when Kolbe was canonized as a martyr by Pope John Paul II on the 10th of October 1982, and a statue to remember this great sacrifice stands above the Great West Door of Westminster Abbey in London.

Kolbe had created his own rule of life as a very young man, much in line with the "Who are you BECOMING?" plan that we are discussing in this book. One of his ten rules:

#6 "Think of what you are doing. Do not be concerned about anything else, whether bad or good."

I stood at the entrance to the cell in which Kolbe was murdered, looking at his picture and the flowers in this cold, dark, tiny space. My body felt weak. What a great man. He understood the questions we discussed earlier: Who am I? What do I stand for? As a result, what will I do with my life? His answers were more surreal and completely flooded over my whole being as I could barely keep my body from collapsing at the entrance to his cell, his place of ultimate sacrifice. Kolbe, like Frankl, knew his why. He lived his why. He gave his life for his why. Could I have chosen to bring forth the same courage that this man had? After touching the place where these two men survived, I knew that I had to get better at making my own choices. I will be forever grateful for their example of finding a why so that you will have the courage to respond to any how.

Chapter 6

Belief

Our actions line up with our beliefs. When we try to act in a way that is incongruent with what we believe to be true about ourselves or the world, we will have a disharmony within. You may recall the discussion of cognitive dissonance from chapter 3. The most likely outcome is that our actions will get back in line with the belief, how we see ourselves and the world.

My kids' fitness business had never done more than 15 parties in a single month, but that was okay. Our green bus team had settled into a comfort zone around delivering this amount of business. I don't know that it was the right time to get uncomfortable. I had done my homework and no other franchise was doing more than this, so this must be what is possible. Who am I to do the impossible? Cognitive dissonance. If the belief is that something is not possible, how can my actions pursue it? We hovered at this 15 parties per bus per month number for over a year. Did I want to do more events? Yes. Could our schedule fit more events? I thought so, at least consciously. Would more people book us? It seemed they wouldn't. Were there more than 15 birthday parties being booked in the 25 mile radius that we served? Absolutely. Over two million people live in that radius. Since we work with children primarily between the ages of 2 and 7, I estimated that about 150,000 people in my radius were potential customers, which meant that about 12,500 birthdays happened in that radius every month. Just by doing these simple calculations, I began to challenge the belief that 15 birthdays each month was about all we could do. The next step was visiting competitors. One of the busiest happened to be doing as many as 25 parties on a single Saturday, and theirs was a stationary location. My dissonance was being shaken up. Their pricing was very similar to ours. If people were driving to this place, they likely would not be traveling much more than about ten miles. This meant my limit was entirely in my head. As Gandhi said, "A person is the center of a circle whose circumference is determined by self-imposed limitations." My belief in what was possible was changed over the course of a few weeks. Let's get to 20 parties every single month became a mantra. And we did. Then 30. Then 50. This change happened very quickly after changing the belief that it was possible.

How often do we see the same change in a sporting event? A college basketball team makes a run and starts building a belief that they can win the game. Football's NY Giants almost beat the New England Patriots in the 2007/2008 regular season. That near

> **"What the mind can conceive and believe, the mind can achieve"**
> **~ Napoleon Hill**

victory fed the Giants' belief and they did beat the Patriots to win the Superbowl. A pitcher starts the first few innings of a game by hitting his spots, getting each pitch in the location he wants, and his belief builds into the later innings. A hitter fouls off a few tough pitches, feeding the belief that this pitcher is hittable. I remember a college basketball game when I hit three consecutive three point baskets in the final minute. That first one fed my belief and I knew the next would go in. I also remember striking out in a key spot in a high school baseball game and repeating that experience in my mind too many times during later at-bats, feeding a counter-productive belief that I would not come through in the clutch.

I think we all realize how powerful our beliefs can be. If I believe that the only way to build a business is to give up everything, sacrifice health, family, and service to others, I will only find answers that fit this model. I will plan to work every weekend, even missing holidays. I will put off personal fitness because that has to wait until my business is built. I say these things because I had believed these things. I had to attack them using the lessons learned from challenging my birthday booking beliefs.

The American Colonists and Belief

The cycle of the body politic – like so many great lessons, this one may not be well-known today, but that doesn't reduce its validity or potency. Alexander Tytler wrote about it approximately 300 years ago. Benjamin Disraeli, considered by many to be one of England's finest prime ministers, discussed it in the late 1800's. Today, I rarely come across someone who has heard of it. The cycle in theory is really quite simple. It says that we go through a cycle, with a bottom and top. On one side of the circle, we are striving. On the other, we are decaying. The "we" reminds me of the quote at the beginning of this section, and includes individuals, families, companies, communities, non-profits, nations, and churches. At the bottom of the cycle, things are not as they need to be. At the top, we've arrived. Green and growing or ripe and rotting. Reflect on the 13 original colonies and this model. The expanded version of the cycle, starting at the bottom, goes from bondage to spiritual faith, spiritual faith to courage, courage to liberty, liberty to abundance (at the peak), abundance to selfishness, selfishness to complacency, complacency to apathy, apathy to dependence, and dependence back to bondage. The original 13 colonies felt they were in bondage to a tyrant. Their spiritual faith led them into courage. This courage fed the fight for freedom and liberty. Liberty was the foundation for abundance. And I will let you decide where our great nation is today. Bondage? Spiritual Faith? Courage? Liberty? Abundance? Selfishness? Complacency? Apathy? Dependence? Where is your organization? Your family? You?

I've reflected on this model quite a bit over the last several years, primarily thinking about the ability to get a person or group of people off the downward side of the cycle. Can it be done? If so, how? "Where there is no vision, the people perish." (Proverbs 29:18) The answer has been around for thousands of years. Get a new vision. Napoleon said that leaders are "dealers in hope." Creating hope for a bigger future is the escape

> "Great minds discuss ideas; average minds discuss events; small minds discuss people."
> ~ Eleanor Roosevelt

route from that downward slope of the cycle. Go dream a new dream. Dream a bigger dream. Dream for your business, for your family, for your nation, for the world. You could probably say that our nation was at the top of the cycle before JFK took office and dreamed a bigger dream. He took us straight to the striving side of the cycle with two challenges. Let's send someone to the moon and back in the next few years. Oh, and let's also ask what we can do for our country, and maybe the world while we're at it. Who's in charge of dreaming bigger dreams for you, personally? I know that I've experienced this cycle many times in my life. I create a vision and chase it down. Then I hit the vision and I've slid part of the way down the decay slope before finding another vision. Without vision, I perish. So do you, my friend, so do you.

From where did the courage spring to pursue the colonists' vision? Spiritual faith. You were built to make a difference. Life's mission is about becoming. Who are you BECOMING today?

Bombard your Mind

Hang gliding on the Outer Banks sand dunes near Kitty Hawk gave me the simultaneous feelings of fast-forwarding to the future of flight and flashing back to December 17, 1903, when Orville and Wilbur dreamed their big dream on that same sand. Of course it seemed necessary that I should belly flop into the sand on my glider, just as they had after that first flight of an incredible 120 feet. I can't say that I consciously planned the belly flop. But it did happen and was worth it!

It was just before the 100 year anniversary of that first manned flight. I had long dreamed of knowing the adventure that Orville and Wilbur pursued, despite so many saying that flight was reserved for birds and angels. I once read that you'll never see a statue erected for a critic. That image helps when there seem to be more critics than supporters. My older brother, Andrew, and I were in North Carolina's Outer Banks for a weekend. It happened to be a race weekend, which we didn't fully understand until we tried to get a hotel as we drove closer to our destination. No openings anywhere. We finally found an out of the way little motel. That Saturday morning, we were on a mission. We *would* learn to hang-glide.

We signed up for a lesson with two parts.

Part one: we would learn to take off, glide, and land. This would happen on the sand dunes, very near and very similar to the dunes on which the Wright Brothers made history.

Part two: at a small grass field airport a few miles away, we would be towed up to 2,000 feet by an ultralight. Part two had us partnered with an experienced hang-glider pilot who would control part of our flight and ensure a safe return to earth. What an experience!

We watched a brief video about take-off, landing, strapping yourself into the glider, and the essentials of turning. Our enthusiastic instructor walked us through some key points. Most of the flight would be very intuitive. Want to go left? Simply think left. You would lean to the left and your weight shift would get the glider to arc to the left. Speed up? Lean forward. Within minutes of the video and instruction, we were experts. That was even before he described landing procedures. It was all so simple that we knew landing had to be common sense. Well... The instructor told us about flaring. Flaring is a way of intentionally stalling the glider, or slowing it enough that it is no longer gliding, but dropping, more like a rigid parachute. Flaring is accomplished by shifting all of the pilot's weight towards the back of the glider. The easy and efficient method is simply accomplished by pushing the glider's bar forward. The further and faster you push it forward, the more abruptly your weight shifts to the back, tilting the glider nose upward and slowing the forward movement until you are dropping instead of flying.

Got it. Simple. Get me on the dunes! Each glider student would get several attempts to launch and land from the dunes. Each flight would only take us about 30 feet above the ground and about as far as 100 yards. Despite our instructors hilarious warnings about "turtleing", one of our classmates performed the art of the turtle perfectly. A turtle move in hang-glider training is best performed when you tilt the glider to one side when flying close to the ground. The end of one wing will catch the sand and flip the glider, with pilot still strapped in, upside down on the sand. Pilot then dangles in the harness, struggling to flip back over or remove the harness. Turtle. The instructor had acted this out at an Emmy level, and we were all hopeful that we might witness this high degree of difficulty landing procedure. One classmate gave us that chance. He was probably the most cautious of the students and didn't run fast on his take off. This low speed kept his glider close to the ground and a small gust must have facilitated the lean. And there he was, upside down *"turtleing"*. He was totally fine, but wiggling and squirming to try to get out of this predicament. What a sight. That was before everyone captured every life moment via video on their phones, otherwise "Kitty Hawk Turtleing" would, without a doubt, be one of those multi-million viewed videos.

After my first two flights I must have been practically convinced that I was Jonathan Livingston Seagull. Flying was all too natural. The instructor would shout out "Flare, Flare, FLARE!" when it was time to stall the glider for a soft landing. If you stall when you are too high or too low, the landing is hard. For my third flight, the headwind had picked up quite a bit and it was starting to drizzle. I knew we might go back inside if the rain became heavier, so I had to make the most of what might be my last flight. I ran as fast as I could to get a great launch. My speed and the strong headwind made the take off easier than before. I felt like the glider rose quite a bit higher than earlier flights and I must have had the biggest grin plastered on my face. I had enough altitude to make some nice turns. Forget seagulls, I'm an eagle. "Flare!" What? Already? No, let's ride this wind! "Flare! Flare!!! FLARE!!!!!" Okay, just a bit. I flared, making the glider nose point upward and slowing my flight path, but then I changed my mind. I really needed to maximize this flight experience. I jerked the glider bar to the opposite position. It was above my head, so I yanked it down to my knees, abruptly shifting my weight towards the nose of the glider, which pointed the glider's nose straight down. This eagle picked up speed and began to fly again like nobody's business – straight into the sand. I've done my share of belly flops into pools, but this was a belly flop like no other. I just lay there, face and front of my body caked with damp sand. Orville and Wilbur got up. Yes, they not only got up, but they frequently had to repair or rebuild a glider after similar miscalculations. You can get up, too. I'm not sure if I got the same applause as our turtle friend, but my classmates were certainly entertained. Oh, if there were videos of that day... The turtle and the belly flop. I can imagine the Wright Brothers having that much fun proving that controlled powered flight was possible.

Just 100 years prior to my glider training, powered flight had never been accomplished. Today, even before my first daughter had turned two, she had flown to the Caribbean, California, Italy, and Poland. Thinking back on that hang-gliding adventure, I wonder what else is possible that we don't attempt. Touching the sand, feeling the wind, running my hand along the track used for that first powered flight – all flooded my mind with a belief that just about anything is possible. I've felt this before and I'm sure you have. We sometimes bombard our mind with things that can happen, evidence of great accomplishments, and our whole being is in a state of complete belief. Belief in humanity. Belief in making the world a better place. Belief in the family. Belief in our selves. Why don't we more intentionally bombard or flood our mind with evidence of what's possible? Napoleon Hill wrote "What the mind can conceive and believe, the mind can achieve." Knowing that the Wright Brothers flew is very different from experiencing their accomplishment, from walking the sand dunes at Kitty Hawk or visiting their bike shop in Dayton, Ohio.

Knowing that Henry Ford put America on wheels is very different from visiting The Henry Ford Museum, walking through the evolution of the automobile, or touring Ford's Greenfield Village and seeing a real Model T drive past Thomas Edison's Menlo Park Laboratory. Knowing that Martin Luther King, Jr. had the courage to stand up for his dream and share it with the world despite the ultimate cost is very

> **"One life is all we have and we live it as we believe in living it. But to sacrifice what you are and to live without belief, that is a fate more terrible than dying."**
> **~ Joan of Arc**

different from standing on the steps of the Lincoln Memorial, envisioning the crowd, and reciting with conviction, "I have a dream that my four little children will one day grow up in a nation where they will not judged by the color of their skin but by the content of their character."

On the day Superstorm Sandy demolished the east coast, I had the chance to do just that. Speaking engagements and closed airports had me driving from Maryland to Charlotte. Just a few hours into this twelve hour journey I was driving, more like floating, through Washington, D.C. Knowing the power of flooding my mind with belief, I decided to stop and visit a few monuments.

First stop: the Jefferson Memorial. In the short run from my car to the monument, I was completely soaked. As I stood in the monument, I reflected on Thomas Jefferson's courage, vision, and belief at the age of 33 to write the Declaration of Independence. Then I thought about the storms that were hitting the nation – not just Sandy, but economic storms, philosophical storms, social storms, spiritual storms. Jefferson's monument was standing up to Sandy. Would his documents, his vision, his nation stand up to the even more destructive storms?

Second stop: Martin Luther King Memorial. As I pulled close to the monument, the rain was so intense that I couldn't really tell if I was on the road. One man walked toward my car. I hoped I hadn't driven on the lawn? The African American gentleman asked if I could give his car a jump. Absolutely. His girlfriend was visiting from out of state and he really wanted her to see the monument! I jumped his car and then splashed over to MLK's monument. Water and tears poured down my face in front of the granite image as I recognized the simple truth that without MLK's dream, the man in need of a jump and I would not have met on this day.

Last stop: Lincoln Memorial. This may be the first time in history that only one person was visiting this landmark. By this point, my water-saturated clothing no longer mattered. As I stood on the steps, I had a thought. Wouldn't it be amazing to stand exactly where MLK stood during the "I have a dream" speech? On the bottom level of the memorial there are two tributes, one to Lincoln and the other to King. I looked through the pictures, videos, and checked online to triangulate King's position. It took several trips out to the steps and back inside to convince me that I had found the right spot. I slowly walked out into the heavy, sideways rain towards *the* spot. Suddenly, I felt the sun and energy of that day, just fifty years ago. The water disappeared. I stopped, looked up and out over the crowd of hundreds of thousands of people. I started speaking:

"I still have a dream. It is a dream deeply rooted in the American Dream. I have a dream that one day this nation will rise up and live out the true meaning of its creed: 'We hold these truths to be self-evident, that all men are created equal.'"

Walking back to my car and throughout the rest of my drive that day, I thought about King visiting India, not only to learn from Gandhi, but to feed his own belief around this dream.

How do you flood your mind with belief? I don't always do it so well, but there is certainly a drastic difference in what I can accomplish when I compare days full of belief to those filled with doubt. Will it take effort? Of course. What's the return on investment, ROI, of investing in building your belief? Henry Ford wisely said, "Whether you think you can or think you can't, either way, you're right." What experiences, stories from history, and inspired people will you surround yourself with in order to build belief?

TFAR

What came first, the chicken or the egg? Thoughts – Feelings – Actions – Results. TFAR. Thoughts lead to feelings. Feelings lead to actions. Actions lead to results. Results affect our thoughts.

Chicken-Egg-Chicken-Egg-Chicken-Egg...
TFAR-TFAR-TFAR-TFAR...

It seems just about everyone I meet wants to make a change in his or her life. They may not tell me of the change, but if I care enough and invest in the relationship, eventually I will hear of substantial changes this unique individual wants to make. You want to make changes. So do I. Why, then, do we so rarely make them? The answer lies in this chicken-egg or T-F-A-R cycle. Which came first? I don't know, nor does it matter in our attempts to make lasting change. If I

> "Sow a thought and you reap an action; sow an act and you reap a habit; sow a habit and you reap a character; sow a character and you reap a destiny."
> ~ Ralph Waldo Emerson

have a chicken, I'm going to get an egg. If I have an egg, I'm going to get a chicken. If I have a certain line of thought, the resulting F-A-R, or feelings, actions, and results, will be fairly predictable. If I have a certain feeling about an issue, the A-R-T will follow. And on and on and on.

To make a true and lasting change, we can interrupt the cycle at any point, but we need to make it through the complete cycle. If I swap the chicken for a robin, I'll get a robin egg, then a robin, then a robin egg, then a robin, then a robin egg... But, if I swap the chicken for a robin, get a robin egg, and then swap a chicken egg back into the cycle, it goes back to Chicken-Egg-Chicken-Egg-Chicken-Egg. This is why we rarely make lasting changes. We try to swap a thought, or even a thought and feeling (I am going to improve this relationship and I believe that it is possible), but then don't keep the cycle going. We don't use our will power to do the actions that a person who has a better relationship would do, don't get the results of a better relationship, and the thoughts and feelings go back to their original "this relationship just isn't working."

Try this out with one change you want to make. Just list the change in terms of each of the categories:

Thoughts – Feelings – Actions – Results

Then get yourself through the cycle a few times. Let's keep using the improved relationship example. To make the relationship with one family member better, you would have to think what? -That this person is important. -That you value this person. -That this person is worthy of your love. What feelings would go with this? You might feel appreciative and that this person is special to you. What actions align? How would you look at this person? What things might you say? Now, what results do you expect? Keep this going around with you being 100% responsible for each of the 4 steps in this cycle. Try it just for today - and maybe again tomorrow.

Who are you BECOMING?

Chapter 7

This Love Thing

Perhaps you have seen an amazing video on YouTube called "Get Service" about a young man that is busily going through his day. Everyone seems to be getting in his way. A boy skateboards in front of the man's car. A woman steals his parking spot. The coffee shop line is too long. Someone in front of him has to add a cookie to his coffee. Delay and inconvenience after delay and inconvenience. Then, something happens that begins to change the whole world of the young man. He is given a pair of glasses that allow him to see the greatest need, challenge, or struggle of each person he looks at. That boy on the skateboard just needed someone to care. A waiter was struggling to overcome addiction. A father had just lost his job and was wondering how he was going to take care of his family. Realizing that each person he encounters has needs, challenges, and problems almost instantly changes the way this young man encounters the world around him.

We all do that. You've seen a movie that helps you realize that others have big struggles, too. As you leave the theater, the barrier between you and the rest of humanity around you has been temporarily lowered. When you and I realize that we're not perfect and that those around us also each have their own imperfections, it suddenly opens the door for us to genuinely love the people around us. The Arbinger Group wrote a great book called *Leadership and Self-Deception*, based partly on psychologist Martin Buber's *I and Thou*. Buber proposed that we can experience two distinct ways of being toward another. We can look at others as objects (vehicles, obstacles, constraints, resources, etc.) or as people (with hopes, dreams, fears, doubts, challenges – just like us). One of the most poignant lessons from *Leadership and Self-Deception* deals with dropping this filter we have towards everyone we meet. How? Two approaches: stop resisting other people and question your own virtue, or perfection. That is exactly what happened to the man after wearing these special

> **"I love mankind - It's people I can't stand!"**
> ~ **Charlie Brown**

glasses in the video. He stopped resisting other people, and instead saw them as people with challenges, just like him. You've felt complete love for another person at some point in your life. And I don't mean just the "in love" feeling. I mean a deep caring for another person. Perhaps it happens often for you. Perhaps it only happens at a funeral or when someone is going through a very tough time. Either way, there are times when you drop that wall, lose the filter, cease resisting that person that crosses your path. For some of us, the hardest ones to do this with are those closest to us. Mother Teresa, after being awarded the Nobel Peace Prize, was asked "What can we do to promote world peace?" Her answer:

"Go home and love your family."

I'm with you, Dadda!

We were just sitting on the couch together. Not watching TV, not reading a book, not doing a puzzle or playing with toys. We were just sitting together. Ella must have been about three and was smiling one of the biggest smiles I have ever seen. An amazing feeling of joy, warmth, happiness, peace, and love seemed to be exuding from her whole being. As a dad, my heart was melted. Finally, I looked down at her and said, "Ella, are you happy?"

"Yes! I'm so happy!"

Time stood still. I waited for what seemed a few weeks and then asked, "Ella, why are you so happy?"

"Dadda, I'm so happy because I'm with you!"

I melted. I'll remember this moment when Ella graduates from kindergarten, first grade, high school, college, when I'm dancing with Ella on her wedding night. I'll remember this moment when, God-willing, I hold my grandchildren someday. I just sat there and tried to hold on to my little girl, hoping that somehow we could just sit together on that couch for a few years. Thank you, Ella, for teaching daddy such an amazing lesson about love.

> **"They love you more than other men do, but they need you less"**
> ~ C.S. Lewis

Sometimes we just need to let love flow into our lives, let it swirl around inside of us gaining energy and power, and then let it flow out of our whole beings. Sometimes we just need to let our love for others be felt by them. Not just a few words or a card or flowers. Really felt.

Many times since then, I have felt the way Ella seemed to feel in that moment. I would go to a quiet church or a quiet place and sit, kneel, or stand, and just feel warmth, joy, peace, happiness, love, safety. I would whisper, "God, I'm so happy because I'm with You!" When I have these moments, I can't help but wonder if God feels something like I did when Ella said those words to me a few years ago. As a parent, I could use more moments like that. As a child of God, I could use more moments like that. God's ready and waiting for His children to sit on his lap. Why don't we do it more often? My friend the monk told me that we can only truly give love when we let ourselves be loved. Brother Antonio would say if you let Him (God) love you then you can't help but love others. It flows into you, swirls around, and flows out towards others. Let Him love you. Let it swirl around, affecting every part of your being, and let it flow towards people in your life.

"It's almost 8 o'clock"

Taking Daddy's little girls swimming at the local YMCA on Friday nights would become a tradition. Remembering so many of the small, but so significant, traditions from my own childhood, I always look for traditions that my own little girls will cherish. Our swimming excursions could be exactly that. Between the plan, that perfect preview video in my mind, and truly living out this fairytale experience lay a barrier of the human condition. Family swim is 6-8 pm. We would often arrive by about 6:45 or 7, just after dinner. Ella loved to find a pair of flippers and demonstrate her dolphin or mermaid swimming capabilities. Maya, at just 2, excitedly jumped back and forth from activity to activity. One moment, she would be collecting every squishy toy animal in the pool; the next Maya would be leaping from poolside into the pool and daddy's arms over and over and over. Next, she might decide to "swim" away, grasping two pool noodles, as I tried frantically to keep up with her newly invented swim style. What amazing moments! Ella often joined the craziness with a game she invented: Daddy chooses a swimming stroke and Ella crosses the pool in that style. We might race, and Ella likes to win every time.

As the hands on the large clock at the shallow end of the pool approached 8:00, I would do what so many of us do. I would move on. I would start thinking about the things that have to get done at home that evening, letting my girls know that it was almost time to go. I began to realize that I was often "checking out" as early as 7:45, shifting my entire focus to what was next and not being fully present with my little mermaid and dolphin. One day, it hit me. I was using the almost 8 o'clock the wrong way. I had made it into a trigger that said time to move on. I made a definitive switch in my mind while standing in the pool that night. I looked at that clock and went through in my mind all the amazing memories that we could create together in the pool. Then I thought of the days when my little girls wouldn't be so little anymore and swimming in the pool in this way would be just a memory. I had what Dr. Izzo describes in *The Five Secrets You Must Discover Before You Die* as a "Rocking Chair Moment." I imagined what I might be thinking someday years into the future reflecting on these pool moments.

What if those last five, ten, or fifteen minutes in the pool were the most amazing part of the memory? Instead of moving on, what if I put everything I had into those last few minutes? I decided that "It's almost 8 o'clock" from that moment forward would be my reminder to create the memory. From that day forward, I would expend every last bit of energy I had in those last few minutes.

> **"Wherever you are, be there."**
> **~ Jim Rohn**

We would motorboat around the pool, do a dolphin jumping game, race backwards underwater, dive to try to reach the bottom, throw Ella and Maya all the way up to the moon and back. I would be there. No moving on. I. Would. Be. There. An amazing speaker, Jim Rohn, used to say, "Where ever you are, be there." "It's almost 8 o'clock" would remind me that where ever I was, I would be there. Knowing that I was making THE memories that would define our Friday swimming trips filled me with energy. Sometimes I even tear up a bit in the pool as the clock approaches 8 o'clock now. I know that there are only so many almost 8 o'clock experiences that each of us get to create. Make each one a special memory. I now repeat that expression quietly to myself often as I am with my family and find myself checking out in anticipation of a project that I am working on. "It's almost 8 o'clock. Make this THE memory!"

Emotional contagion

I was holding a two-year-old upside down, helping him attempt his first flip on the rings in one of my big green buses. Everything was going perfectly. He may have been a bit nervous, but a big grin was working its way across his face. His feet touched the ceiling and we paused, so that he could show mommy, who was standing in the front of the bus conversing with a friend. Our future Olympian finally got his mother's attention and, within a tenth of a second, the whole scene was transformed. The little boy was no longer smiling, he was now bawling, petrified, and wanted to be handed to MOMMY. Not only that, but an anxious, nervous tension had spread throughout the bus, and several of the young birthday party guests were now singing the "Mommy" song with a strange harmony that shouldn't be heard by any newlyweds who still think having children is a good idea.

What created this change? One look from the mother's eyes had transferred an emotional message directly into that little boy. The emotions: fear and cowardice. Message received and applied.

Haven't we all experienced this emotional contagion? In my green buses, I've seen hundreds of incidents like this. I've researched and spoken on the topic of Emotional Intelligence, and this scenario comes from a unique feature in our brains called mirror neurons. Our brains like to mirror what is seen, heard, felt by others, especially effective when a strong emotion comes from a parent to a child while making eye contact. It happens with all sorts of emotions. Courage can be transferred. Love. Doubt. Fear. Anxiety. Not just can they all be transferred, they ARE all transferred – and very effectively. Do we use this for the positive? Sometimes some of us do. We all do it for the negative at times.

I encourage you to explore this from the perspective of many different emotions and many different scenarios. Let's just look at it from a love and acceptance perspective. So often we go into a difficult conversation with someone, investing time to think through the words we should use and the issues we should address. When is the last time you invested that same amount of time working through the feelings you should have for that person

> "We can complain because rose bushes have thorns, or rejoice because thorn bushes have roses."
> ~ Abe Lincoln

as you deliver your message? Long after people forget what we say, they will remember how they felt around us. Try this simple exercise. Pick one person; one of your children, your spouse, a sibling, a parent. Focus on that person and think only about the positives of that person. How can you build up an overpowering feeling of love, concern, acceptance, and appreciation for this person that swirls around inside of you, affecting every part of your being? Then, in every communication with that person over the next week, build that feeling before, during, and after the communication. Let that overpowering feeling of love flow out of you towards them. You should be able to feel it and see how it affects their state.

Create the emotional contagion. Use applied teach-ability. Experiment. Get feedback. One of the greatest magicians of the 20th century used to look at himself in the mirror before every act and repeat the phrase, "I love my audience! I love my audience!" He would then list all the reasons he was grateful for his audience and take the stage. He truly felt love for his audience and they loved him right back. People can feel what you feel towards them. Practice love. It's been called the most powerful force in the world. Love conquers all. Isn't it about time we got good at it?

This love theory meets the real world

I don't think you and I are that different. Even as I write about this love thing, I can't help but think about its application or lack-thereof in the real world. Good luck with that one. I hear you loud and clear. Those were my exact sentiments just a few short years ago. Then I did what so many theorists and philosophers do. I built this little theory in my mind without having to try it out for myself under challenging circumstances. It reminds me of a common request: quite often I am asked to incorporate an ethics component into leadership programs. A seminar attendee in Edison, NJ, told me that he used to work for Enron. He went on to share that any of us, if reading the case study of Enron, would say that we would never have done what was done. Reading case studies can be very similar to my theorizing.

This love theory would be very different. I would get a great chance to test this one out.

In depth discussions had gone on for about a year. The manager of my green bus business would buy the business. I will call him Mitch. This was part of my journey to move on in life. We had yet to settle on a final price, timing, or terms of the buyout, but the business sale was moving forward. Then everything changed. Our manager was no longer interested. It was midsummer, the business was very busy, and suddenly the manager didn't want to buy our business. I had invested a tremendous amount of time in training him to do each and every piece of the business; marketing, sales, hiring, training, payroll, finances, and maintenance. He knew the business inside and out. What to do and what not to do. From working with so many small businesses, I had come to the conclusion that there are about a half dozen "secrets" that really make each small business work. Learning which marketing buttons to push versus not push was worth a few years and thousands of dollars of our investment. That was one of this business's secrets. My manager knew all the secret recipes. Who to hire, how to hire; where, when, and what to post for the best application responses. How to effectively weed out those who don't have the character traits to excel in our customer experience.

It was July. Mitch was no longer interested, not even in negotiating. Over the next two months, both of our bus motors blew up. Blew up might seem like a harsh over-exaggeration, but that's about what happened with two bus motors. Two motors that would never run again. We were busy year round by this point, and it was a mad dash to get one of the buses back on the road without losing too many customers. What exactly happened to the motors, we will never completely know. Did they overheat from a cooling problem? Were they extremely low on oil or coolant? Did they suddenly lose coolant or was it very low? The bus mechanical logs didn't show any signs of being low on oil or coolant, but the coincidental loss of both motors stirred concern over the integrity of the maintenance process and logs. The drama that summer was just the beginning. In December, our two key people casually let us know that neither would be available in January. The manager said he was going back to his old job from several years ago. The other key person said he was getting married, going back to school full time, and might be moving. Then, I found out. Talk about a serious frying pan moment. It was just the first week in January and I was bringing newly hired staff to one of our clients. The sign was blatant. It was posted on the front lawn of the daycare. A different bus was scheduled to visit this daycare, and a big picture of that bus was plastered on the sign in the front lawn. What? Later that same day, one of our long time customers pulled me aside and asked if we were closing, selling, or going out of business. No. Why? She then informed me that my manager, Mitch – the person I had trained to do everything, the person we had paid even when the business couldn't quite cover his pay, the person who stopped negotiating purchase of the business just a few weeks before two engines blew up – had informed this customer that he was taking over the business with a different bus because we were selling or going out of business or changing names. The customer told me that it sounded too suspicious, so she waited to discuss with me.

Over the next few days, it would get progressively worse. Mitch had contacted most, if not all, of our customers over many months, letting them know about this "transition" of ownership. The sale of the business was going to help facilitate my transition into the next phase – closer to the pursuit of my overlapping three circles (TPS). Now, I had lost some customers and paid a significant price to tow buses and replace motors. What would I do? Advice came rapidly and intensely. Sue him. File a "cease and desist" order. Publicize his theft. Find his bus. What would you recommend? Not many said to forgive him. I could lie to you and say that I didn't feel tempted to go after this crime from many angles. This was a dilemma. Forgive. Love. Or a more "realistic" business solution? The price was so much more than financial. I had lost so much time that was to be dedicated towards serving in the ways that I was built to serve. Now I would have to get back involved in the day-to-day operations of the business as we tried to rebuild. Revenge had such a nice sound to it. But I was not supposed to be about revenge. Love and forgiveness was the theory. Stealing from my business, from my family, and from my time to make a difference in the world was the reality. What should I do? God, what do you think I should do? That became my question. And when I allowed that question to permeate my thinking, a calm peace accompanied the answer. Forgive. Love. I can't say

> "Let your religion be less of a theory and more of a love affair."
> ~ G. K. Chesterton

that I always focused on that question or that I always wanted to hear that answer. It wasn't long before I drove past the parking spot of my new competitor's bus. Then I found that he was using the exact same approach that I had taught him to market his new business online. How many would be tempted to let the air out of his tires, drain the oil, disconnect the batteries, something – anything – to feel close to getting even. I can't tell you that some of these thoughts didn't work their way into my mind at times. Make the bigger question the dominant question. "God, what do you think I should do?" Then, I continued the conversation. "God, if that's what you want me to do, please help me to do it!" Because I don't always feel like making that choice.

Who am I BECOMING? More loving? More forgiving? More selfless? Or more vengeful, more spiteful, more bitter, more angry? My bus experience may never happen to you, but things will happen that require a similar response. If I hadn't decided ahead of time that this "Who am I BECOMING?" question should be central to my life, and that Loving and Forgiving were part of the answer, this experience would have left me open to many more options. Recall my wife's grandparents in Poland telling me that they sheltered Jews from the Nazis, as if there were no other option. This is the fruit of right thinking, of having the right questions or pillars at the center of our lives. So many decisions become obvious. There is no other way to go. Revenge is not aligned with who I am becoming. Is it aligned with who you are becoming?

My friend, the monk, was kind enough to offer a valuable perspective on this. Decide, he informed me over some Italian wine and *Zuppa di Pesce*, comes from the Latin *decidere*, which means to cut off or cut away. Decide is to cut off other alternatives, to cut away other options. Once "Loving" is something that I have decided to become, I must cut off other alternatives. Otherwise, I have not truly decided. Brother's wisdom: "Jonathan, tell me about some of your decisions." I pass his wisdom on to you. My dear friend, tell me about some of your decisions.

Walt chooses Mickey over Bitterness

A story behind the story from Walt Disney's early life has inspired me and kept me on course many times. Walt often reminded the world that "it all started with a mouse." Well, before that mouse, there was a not quite as well-known lucky rabbit by the name of Oswald. The Disney studio made this cartoon series as their bread and butter for a few years and it had been gaining in national popularity. In late February of 1928, a 26-year-old Walt made the long train trip from California to New York to re-negotiate the distribution contract for the crown jewel of the Disney Studios, this lucky rabbit. Walt was met in NY with a demand to lower, not raise, the price on each rabbit cartoon. Then the distributor, Charles Mintz, played his trump card. He owned the rights to the rabbit (standard practice at the time) and had hired practically all of Walt Disney's staff away from

> "The moment a person forms a theory, his imagination sees in every object only the traits which favor that theory."
> ~ Thomas Jefferson

the Disney Studios. Walt was offered a job working for Mintz. Either way, Walt's staff would continue making Oswald cartoons, with or without Walt. Could this really be happening? A call to Roy Disney, who was back in California, confirmed that almost the entire staff were resigning. How could this be? Walt had taught them the art of animation. He had paid his animators quite well, more than he paid himself. There are many turning points, defining moments, in each of our lives. Truth be told, turning points happen each and every day. Something doesn't go our way. We can choose to get bitter or better. We can borrow from Napoleon Hill, who put Andrew Carnegie's success philosophy into a formula when writing *Think and Grow Rich*. One of Hill's famous phrases: "within every adversity there is a seed of equal or greater benefit." What would Walt do about Oswald? The night Walt departed NY for the return trip to California, his telegram to Roy included these words: "DON'T WORRY EVERYTHING OK".

What was okay? The only money maker for the studio was gone. So was the team that created the cartoon. Walt Disney had retired from drawing cartoons three years earlier because he just wasn't that good at it. How would all be okay?

Walt could have sunken into a pit of despair. He could easily have thrown in the towel. His dreams could have ended that winter day in New York. On the train ride back to California, Walt created a little mouse, whose name would start out as Mortimer and quickly change to Mickey. Mickey Mouse would make his world debut just a few short months later in Steamboat Willie. A Mouse that would impact most of the modern world. The seed of an equal or greater benefit.

Haven't we all experienced moments when our "Oswald the Lucky Rabbit" was taken from us? Bitter or better? Resentment or a quest for the seed of an equal or greater benefit?

My wife and I like the expression "bitterness and resentment is like you drinking poison and expecting the other person to die." Every now and then, one of us will be holding onto some bitterness. The other will make a motion as if drinking something, sound out "glug, glug, glug" and then say "die, die, die" to dramatize the effect of this bitterness. What if Walt spent that train ride thinking about bitterness instead of creating the mouse?

All of this, but I knew. I knew...

There's a legend worth sharing. It has helped me through this process and I think it will serve you.

A young boy was walking along a path in the woods when he came across a rattlesnake. The boy froze in his tracks, but the rattlesnake, who was getting old, smiled at the little boy and softly made his request, "Please, little boy, carry me to the mountaintop. I would so like to see the sunset just one last time before I die." The little boy knew that this was a rattlesnake and replied "Mr. Rattlesnake, I'm sorry. I can't take you. If I pick you up, you will surely bite me and I'll die."

The rattlesnake's reply: "Little boy, I promise that I will not bite you. Won't you grant an old snake one final request? Please take me up the mountain." The little boy thought and thought before he finally picked up the rattlesnake, held it close to his chest, and carried it up the mountain. Together they sat, experiencing the sun's majestic evening display. After sunset the rattlesnake broke the silence, "Little boy, you are so kind. Thank you. Can we go home now? I am tired, and I am old." The little boy picked up the rattlesnake and carried him all the way down the mountain to his home to

> "In theory there is no difference between theory and practice. In practice there is."
> ~ Yogi Berra

die. Just before the little boy laid the rattlesnake down, the rattlesnake turned and bit him in the chest. The little boy screamed in pain, threw the snake upon the ground, and leapt back. "Why? Mr. Snake, why? Why did you do that? Now I will surely die!" The rattlesnake grinned wearily as he looked up at the little boy, "You knew what I was when you picked me up."

You knew what I was when you picked me up.

A frying pan. A rattlesnake. How many things in my life did I keep picking up, even though I knew exactly what they were?

Who am I becoming? More or less loving? More or less forgiving? Better or worse at judging character? Better or worse at knowing myself? More or less willing to say no to good, say no to distractions, in order to say yes to great and yes to a worthy purpose?

Chapter 8

Where will you go from here?

Don't hide minivans!

Corporate America must have a different set of rules. This recipe of "Who are you BECOMING?" need not apply in that world, right? I may have been in for one of the most resounding frying pan moments of my life.

The Detroit suburbs seem to be owned by the Big Three automotive companies. Rick was a relatively new plant manager for one of the Big Three, having been recruited about a year prior from Toyota, with the hopes that he could help bring Toyota, lean, kaizen, and a team culture to a traditional factory. On one of my visits to his plant, Rick called me aside and asked for help figuring out his biggest challenge. "We all agreed [the management team for a ~2,000 person facility] to implement one tool from Toyota's arsenal about a month ago," Rick explained. "We installed Stop Buttons on the final assembly line so that each worker could stop the whole line if quality was not up to par." Perhaps you recall an advertisement by Toyota several years ago depicting a STOP BUTTON and stating that any operator could stop the manufacturing line if quality was not what it should be. The team would then have to fix the cause of the quality issue. Simple idea. While it creates a focus on quality, it could be difficult to fix the issue. Rick's management team had agreed to give it a shot. In this meeting, a month after this decision, Rick described his visit to *gemba* (Japanese for "where the action happens"), the factory floor, that week.

> *"I walked through the final assembly area, realizing that we had not been stopping the line much lately. Then I walked to neighboring sections of the factory, until I entered a warehouse that we were not currently using, a large, quiet, dark, empty warehouse. As I entered, I realized that it was large, quiet, and dark, but not empty. That warehouse was completely full of cars – hundreds, probably close to 500 cars – all built within the last few days, all with the same defect. We had NOT been stopping the line. With a little research, I found that the operators didn't even know why the new stop buttons had been installed."*

Who was lying to whom? The leadership team of this factory was fixing the defects with overtime each weekend. To whom were they lying? Philosopher Eric Hoffer said, "We lie loudest when we lie to ourselves."

Why would they lie?

I shared this story with a business partner who also happened to be my older brother, Andrew. I thought it was just another funny story about some of those things "they" do – the ambiguous "they" representing big companies, generic people, or anyone else who does "that" kind of thing. My brother asked a tremendous question that brought me hurling back from "they" to "me". As we laughed, Andrew asked, "Where are *WE* hiding 500 minivans in our business?" Oh. Wasn't ready for that. We wouldn't hide minivans, would we? Of course we would and of course we were. What challenges or problems keep re-occurring that we either hide or pretend don't exist? Perhaps we fix them on overtime on the weekends. Or hire extra people to keep taking care of the same issue. Or take time away from our families repeatedly to patch up the same problem over and over and over again. Or lose potential business because of a "hidden minivan" in the customer experience.

We were hiding minivans in our business; the only question was where? Then my thoughts went down the path... Where am I hiding 500 minivans in my life? Relationships? Leadership? Business? Health? Emotional well-being? Spirituality?

How about you? Maybe it's only 200 minivans or 50 minivans. Maybe it's 2,500.

Where do you hide minivans?

While you ponder that, let's explore another part of an automotive company. This facility makes vehicles for the high profile luxury brand. At the end of the production line, most cars head off to dealerships, but an occasional VIP vehicle is tagged and sent to a very interesting part of the facility. I wandered through this VIP part of the plant and my curiosity was peaked. One section was

> "We lie loudest when we lie to ourselves."
> ~ Eric Hoffer

individual car stalls with lighting like a professional football stadium, all sorts of tools and parts bins, and mirrors on the floor. The quality inspector would go through every aspect of these VIP vehicles as if autopsying them. Many slight repairs and adjustments were made to ensure that nothing was loose, wind noise was eliminated, doors opened and closed like butter, etc. These truly were VIP cars. I had to ask the question. Where do these VIP cars go? To company executives was the frank reply.

Why? We wouldn't want them driving a vehicle that had any issues. Oh wow. I couldn't think of any other response in the moment. More minivans, only these were luxury vehicles. We lie loudest...

If we're to make serious progress on this "Who are you BECOMING?" journey, you and I need to find ways to effectively and regularly unhide our minivans. Will you do it? Let me share one example.

I enjoy food. Okay, I really like food. Most of it.

A few years ago, I had somehow gained about 30 pounds that didn't belong to me. How I did it is still a mystery. Well, those minivans are going to stay hidden. How did I get rid of those 30 pounds? I shed light on the minivans on a regular basis. I had heard of a study about dieting that tried to analyze what people who lost significant weight and kept it off had in common. One of the driving factors: select a target weight and constantly check in to see where you are. So I began weighing myself every single day and tracking it into a spreadsheet. The next thing I did, which was most effective for me: 3 sets of 8 pull-ups on a regular basis. I couldn't do the pull-ups if I was too heavy or not in the regular habit of doing them. This forced consistency and attention to diet. Also, I could do pull-ups anywhere. They take almost no time. No excuses and measurable feedback. I got a pull-up bar for my house. I'm often seen doing pull-

> "When I find myself in times of trouble, Mother Mary comes to me..."
> ~The Beatles

ups hanging from playground swings while my little girls play nearby, or hanging from a tree branch on a walking route. I don't know what your minivans are. I don't know the best way for you to unhide them. But you do. And you'll find the best way to unhide them. Email me at JFanning@JonathanFanning.com if you're struggling with this and we can figure it out together. My simple strategy of 3 sets of 8 pull-ups effectively helped me drop 30 pounds and keep it off. As I write this, I am reminded that I can do a few more pull-ups between chapters. I will be right back! "Don't hide minivans!" ~Anonymous

1 set of footprints

Well, I have found myself in what often felt like much more than my share of troubled times.

The poem by Mary Stevenson has helped me tremendously.

Footprints in the Sand

One night I dreamed I was walking along the beach with the Lord.
Many scenes from my life flashed across the sky.
In each scene I noticed footprints in the sand.
Sometimes there were two sets of footprints,
Other times there were one set of footprints.

This bothered me because I noticed
That during the low periods of my life,
When I was suffering from anguish, sorrow or defeat,
I could see only one set of footprints.

So I said to the Lord,
"You promised me Lord,
That if I followed you,
You would walk with me always.
But I have noticed that during
The most trying periods of my life

Where will you go from here?

There have only been one set of footprints in the sand.
Why, when I needed you most,
You have not been there for me?"

The Lord replied,
"The times when you have
Seen only one set of footprints,
Is when I carried you."

Walt's last, biggest, and unrealized dream

On December 15, 1966, Disneyland remained open and many flocked there in tears, mourning the death of the creator of this magical place. Who dreams of creating a magical land where there is "no chipped paint and all the horses jump"? In the 1930's, Walt would often take his two daughters to Griffith park, a small park across the street from his Hyperion Studio. As the girls would ride the old carousel, Walt would sit on a green park bench, watching the joyous magic of childhood. As a dad, I can imagine the feeling: you're swept away and want to hold that moment forever. The ride would slow down and Walt would get up to greet his little horseback princesses. The magic of the moment would fade as this dad noticed that many of the horses didn't move and most had chipped or faded paint. The seed of a vision was growing roots and beginning to blossom. What if there were a place where the magic didn't fade? What if there were a place with no chipped paint and all the horses jumped? What if? What if... So many of us experience similar park bench moments, where we dream of what might be. Maybe it's a dream of things we'll do, an impact we'll make, adventures we'll live, the memories we'll create, the relationships we'll build, the person we'll become. But then we don't always feed and water that seed of a vision. Walt fed and watered it, fed and watered it, fed and watered it, and created Disneyland two decades later. His daughters would later recall asking Daddy to stop talking about this dream because it was too unbelievable and it just kept growing and growing.

Two months before dying from lung cancer, Walt would share with the world an even bigger dream. A vivid dream that he had been feeding and watering for quite some time. You may have heard little bits of the dream, but this dream has not come to pass. Walt Disney's last, biggest, and unrealized dream. In October of 1966, Walt was in the studio recording his vision for this dream. The filming was interrupted several times as Walt's coughing spells would overtake the visionary. Several times, he had to be administered oxygen. If you watch the film today, you wouldn't realize that the tour guide was just two months shy of breathing his last breath.

Walt Disney exuded passion and energy as he outlined this dream. The dream was about a living, breathing city. Experimental Prototype Community of Tomorrow. EPCOT in capital letters. But not the Epcot that you and I are familiar with. The EPCOT Walt would describe in detail that October was a city that would house between 60,000 and 100,000 people. The city would be self-sufficient in every way. This would be the first city in the world with no pollution, no crime, and no traffic. Personal electric monorail cars on a series of elevated tracks would take you from where you were to where you wanted to be, without a driver. Homes would be energy self-sufficient. Everything that came into your home would be recyclable. Educational systems would be decades ahead of the current standard. How would Disney do this? The same way he had approached every dream. The dream started small, but Walt fed and watered it over many years. He had studied city design in great depth and was starting to gather a team of the best in the world for this impossible dream. You have to understand that Walt had heard the word impossible so many times before that the word no longer frightened him. His reply: "It's fun to do the impossible!" Walt had already been granted permission from the Florida legislature to establish a separate governing district for this Community of Tomorrow.

A few weeks after recording this video, Walt would tell his son-in-law, Ron Miller, in reference to this new dream, "If I had 15 more years, I would surpass all that I've done in the last 45." But he didn't have 15 more years. On December 15, 1966, Walt would leave this world. He left it very different than he found it. Older brother, Roy, would stick with the "Florida Project" until the Magic Kingdom was completed. Roy passed away just two months after opening day and Card Walker took over as CEO. EPCOT plans had been temporarily put on hold, but when the project plans were presented to Roy Disney just months after

> "Tomorrow is just a dream away."
> ~ Walt Disney

Walt's passing, Roy's response was simple and telling, "Walt's dead." And so was EPCOT. For half a dozen years after Walt's death, a model of this dream was on display at Disneyland in California. In 1974, Disney's then CEO Card Walker announced that the company was reconsidering EPCOT, from a market, technology, economics, and operations perspective. A marvelous theme park called Epcot, not E.P.C.O.T., opened in October of 1982, 16 years after Walt made that video. The park amazed guests then and now, but it is not the living, breathing E.P.C.O.T. - "Experimental Prototype Community of Tomorrow" - that Walt envisioned as a beacon to the world of what a community could be. As my understanding of the magnitude of this dream grew, my response went from hope to anger, disgust, disappointment, and then back to hope. What a bold dream! How could "they" not finish this dream? Why? The world is in such dire need of a beacon of hope. Like so many great dreams, whatever the scale, whether world-altering or simply changing the course of a single person's day, without you or I or Walt to make it happen, the dream will not happen.

Author and Orlando Magic COO, Pat Williams, wrote this in his brilliant book *How to be Like Walt*:

"We shouldn't be too hard on Walt's successors for not building Walt's city of the future. It may have been wise, after Walt died, to downsize his dream. The Disney Company, after all, is a public company, and has a responsibility to its shareholders. Trying to build Walt's dreams without Walt himself to energize those dreams might have been a disaster."

Walter Disney Miller, Walt's grandson, said, "EPCOT was my grandfather's biggest dream – the city of the future that would point the way to a better world. His dream remains unbuilt. When he died, the company lost the driving personality that focused the organization's energies on a single goal." Williams added, "The world lost its tour guide to the future." Every time I think about Walt's last, biggest, and unrealized dream, it leads me down a path that is central to this whole book and life, itself. Without Walt to finish the dream, it didn't happen. You and I have dreams that may just be seedlings right now. But the truth, both energizing and frightful, is simply this: if you don't make that dream happen, it won't. If you don't make it happen, it will not happen. People whose lives your dream would impact – they just won't be impacted. The lasting impact on the world around you – if you don't do it, that impact won't happen. Perhaps many of your dreams have been put on hold or buried. Dig them up. Figure out what one or two of your significant dreams are. Once you have a meaningful dream identified, hunt it down. If you don't chase it, it won't happen. Your dreams are not your dreams by accident. The world needs you to answer the call. Now is your time.

Who are you BECOMING?

About the Author

Jonathan Fanning is the author of several books, including *I Once Was Lost* and *Creativity Unleashed!* He has inspired and challenged audiences with his message around the world. He speaks for companies, non-profits, educational organizations, and churches. Jonathan was voted the best speaker at a recent TED conference. A traumatic car accident and several other "Frying Pan" moments in the middle of Fanning's career as a management consultant launched a quest for a deeper sense of purpose, meaning, and significance. *"Who are you BECOMING?"* and *"Who are you helping the people around you to BECOME?"* became central to Jonathan's life, business, and speaking. He has built several successful businesses, including a national children's fitness franchise and Entrepreneur Adventure, which helps young people experience business start-up and ownership. Jonathan lives in NY with his wife and daughters.

Our popular speeches, workshops & coaching programs include:
- *Who are you BECOMING?*
- *Creativity Unleashed: 5 Habits of World-Class Innovators*
- *The Servant Leader Paradox: Leaders we CHOOSE to Follow and Cultures we CHOOSE to Join*
- *Developing Emotional Intelligence*

Visit us online for more information and to join our free "Who are you BECOMING? Challenges"!

www.JonathanFanning.com

Made in the USA
Middletown, DE
24 November 2023

43363214R00106